£3,-
ge

NINE-YEAR-OLDS
GROW UP

NINE-YEAR-OLDS
GROW UP

A follow-up study of schoolchildren

Sheila Mitchell

TAVISTOCK
London and New York

First published in 1987
by Tavistock Publications Ltd
11 New Fetter Lane, London EC4P 4EE

Published in the USA by
Tavistock Publications
in association with Methuen, Inc.
29 West 35th Street, New York NY 10001

© 1987 Sheila Mitchell

Typeset by Scarborough Typesetting Services
and printed in Great Britain at
the University Press, Cambridge

British Library Cataloguing in Publication Data
Mitchell, Sheila
Nine-year-olds grow up: a follow-up
study of schoolchildren.
1. Personality – Case studies
2. Child psychology – Case studies
I. Title
155.2'34   BF698

ISBN 0–422–78970–4

Library of Congress Cataloging in Publication Data
Mitchell, Shelia, 1926–
Nine-year-olds grow up.

Includes indexes.
1. Buckinghamshire – Social conditions.
2. Children – England – Buckinghamshire – Social conditions.
3. Children – England – Buckinghamshire – Longitudinal
studies.   I. Title.
HN398.B83M58   1987   305.2'34'094259   86–30039

ISBN 0–422–78970–4

CONTENTS

ACKNOWLEDGE-MENTS

I wish to acknowledge my great indebtedness to the many people who have played some part, often a vital one, in facilitating the work which forms the basis of this book. These include (in chronological order): the Social Science Research Council for financial backing between 1977 and 1980, Derek Jackson and Ann Fehilly for their help in planning, piloting, and organizing the fieldwork; the interviewers who, in many cases, put quite exceptional effort into tracing and contacting potential respondents; the administration of St John's Hospital for temporary shelter; the NHS Central Register at Southport and all health authorities (particularly those covering Buckinghamshire and Berkshire) for helping us to contact the 'untraceable' cases; Peter Rosa for his invaluable help in organizing the computer analysis of the data (1978–80) and for the continuing encouragement and help in working out problems which he has provided since funding ceased; Sheena Fraser for her accurate and cheerful help with the analysis; Dorothy Anderson, Moira Taylor, and, particularly, Rachel Haigh for their ability to transform messy drafts into pristine typescript; Michael Shepherd for his encouragement of an often very reluctant author; Gill Davies of Tavistock for her patience. Most important of all, however, are those people who gave so generously of their time and attention – those who agreed to be interviewed, and those who completed and returned our bulky postal questionnaire. It is to these, our informants, that my most fervent thanks are due because, without them, there would truly have been no book.

Sheila Mitchell
May 1986

— 1 —————————

INTRODUCTION

WHY THE BOOK WAS WRITTEN

What will become of them? This must be one of the most frequently experienced thoughts of adults looking at their own
children and those of others. Will that little girl, competently
organizing her playmates, use those same talents to become a
business tycoon? Is the disobedient, troublesome 'terror' of the
school class likely to end up in prison? What of this nice 'normal'
child with no particular talents or defects? Are there any clues
which will help us see into the future?

Unfortunately, despite its intrinsic interest, this remains an area
in which 'prediction' tends, in the main, to reflect the views of the
person making the prediction as to how the social world operates
and how individuals develop. It is generally accepted that there *is*
a link between childhood personality and/or experiences (which,

of course, may themselves be related) and the way in which the individual's life develops. The nature of the relationship, however, can be seen in many different ways according to the orientation of the viewer. So, among theories influential at some time in the last hundred years, we can find that 'success' in life (or lack of it) has been attributed to one or more of the following: heredity/genetic constitution; antenatal and paranatal experiences; nutrition in childhood; quality of the parent–child relationship; the amount of stimulation provided by the environment in early years; parental attitudes towards education; the social status of the parental home in relation to access to resources; the social and economic characteristics of the area in which children spend their formative years; the characteristics of the school attended; the way in which different categories of children are perceived by influential adults (for example, teachers, policemen, employees). If such factors present a 'favourable' picture then chances of success in life (however that may be defined) are seen as good: if 'unfavourable', the outlook is bleaker.

Many studies – too many, indeed, to provide a manageable bibliography – have examined these relationships. Usually they have concentrated on one particular set of factors – for example the association between the presence of books in the home and acquisition of reading skills in school or, ranging more widely, that between the educational and occupational successes of children and their fathers' occupational status.

Relatively few studies have looked at adult 'careers' (in the broadest sense rather than purely in terms of occupation) in relation to the attributes of the individuals themselves rather than those of their homes and parents. Furthermore, those who have attempted to establish such associations have often been obliged to rely on retrospective descriptions of what had occurred. For example, they might start with a group of people with 'a problem' in adult life (such as child abusers, alcoholics, or schizophrenics) and by questioning them, their parents, their old teachers, and so on, try to find out whether they had shown any atypical characteristics when they were younger. Even if some control was kept over the exercise by using a comparable group (in terms of age, sex, social background) of 'normal' people, such studies are still open to criticism. The main problem is that it is not only the investigators who may expect to find a relationship between present 'problem' and past happenings, but also the people being questioned may do so. They may therefore see the past through a filter of what they now know about the individual concerned. If so, they may pick out for mention those events and items of behaviour which fit best with what has happened and with their own picture of *why* it happened.

If we want to relate the characteristics of a person as a child to those of the same person later in life without allowing this kind of 'interpretation' to creep in, we have to obtain *contemporary* information – that is to ask our earlier questions while the subjects of our survey are still children. Sometimes this can be done at a later date by using contemporary records made by schools, hospitals, courts, and other such agencies. This means, however, that we have to rely on information gathered for another purpose: it may not answer all the questions we would like to ask.

The alternative – to gather our own information when the subjects of our study are children and again later – has clear methodological advantages but poses administrative problems. Longitudinal studies, in which the same people are studied in detail fairly continuously over a period of years, provide an excellent basis for mapping events as they happen and tracing the development of specific themes in individual biographies. Such studies are, however, extremely expensive to operate. To allow for adequate coverage of minority groups which may emerge only later (for example, those affected by alcohol abuse or broken marriages) the numbers initially encompassed must be large. Keeping track of those involved, gathering information at intervals, processing the data gathered – all these require the employment of an adequate staff for a substantial period of time. In view of the funding required, the dearth of such programmes is hardly surprising.

More manageable, and much cheaper, is the type of study in which an attempt is made to follow up after a period of years those people who were studied comprehensively in respect of some aspects of their lives. By returning to these people later we cannot trace developments as they occur as would be possible with a longitudinal study but we can, by looking at the same person at two different points in time, see if our earlier information provides any clues to subsequent events. This is the approach followed in the present study.

In 1976 the complete records of a comprehensive survey of children's behaviour, carried out in 1961, were recovered from storage. Could these be used to test the predictive power of information collected about children at one particular point in their childhood? By tracing these children (now grown-up) and finding out what had happened to them would we find that those with many reported 'behaviour problems' as children had developed into more problem-ridden adults than those with few? Were particular types of childhood behaviour forerunners of specific adult 'successes' or 'disasters'?

It was with this aim that the research project was initiated. As the work proceeded, however, it became clear that, in addition, we were producing a picture of what it was like to grow up in the affluent south-east of Britain in the 1960s and reach adulthood in the 1970s.

Such information has its own value. Our knowledge of contemporary life rests on three main sources: our own experience, the pictures presented by the media, and, less impressionistically, the information collected by government departments and other agencies in relation to their administrative needs. Of these, the first two provide a detailed personal picture but give no assurances about the typicality of what is happening (and, indeed, media reports tend to relate to the 'interesting', in other words the atypical). 'Official' statistics on the other hand show clearly what proportion of the population does what (for example, in terms of education, employment, earnings, expenditure, family composition, housing) but, because they relate to entire populations, do not usually attempt to show how these various aspects of people's lives hang together in terms of individual families or individuals.

In this study we can take up an intermediate ground. While our group is large enough to move out of the 'case history' category, by looking at different aspects of the lives of the *same* people we can also say something about the ways in which various aspects of life interrelate with each other.

Indeed, as analysis of our data proceeded it became evident that it was this type of interrelation which was of increasing importance. Because of this, the form of the book has changed from that originally envisaged. Instead of a straight comparison between the 1961 data and those collected in 1978, we have also carried out a great deal of cross-analysis on the 1978 data. In doing so we have had to abandon some of our 'principles' – for example, in terms of accepting retrospective data in relation to such matters as number of jobs held, qualifications gained at school, hospital admissions, court appearances, and so on. This may have introduced some distortion but we feel that if it has done so, it is to a relatively marginal extent. For example, the person with many jobs may forget one or two but will still appear as one of an 'extreme' group for comparison with those for whom a job change is such an atypical event as to be clearly recalled.

THE ORIGINAL (1961) DATA

In 1961 a large-scale survey, financed by the Nuffield Provincial Hospitals Trust, was carried out in what was then the local administrative area of Buckinghamshire.[1] This study was designed to examine the prevalence of behaviour disorders among school-age children and also to establish what was 'normal' behaviour (in the statistical sense) for children of a given age and sex. To this end, questionnaires dealing with behaviour, health,

---

[1] Owing to redrawing of boundaries, this included areas such as Slough which now lie in other administrative areas.

and family background were sent to the parents of a one-in-ten random sample of pupils of statutory school age (that is aged between five and fifteen years) attending local authority schools in the same area and of those, 93 per cent were returned completed. At the same time, separate questionnaires were sent to schools to be completed by each sample child's class teacher, leading to educational information becoming available for nearly all (97 per cent) of our subjects.

The information parents were asked to provide about their children's behaviour was of two main types:

1   A series of twenty-two triple-choice questions on behaviour traits as measured by the parent's estimate of intensity of behaviour (extreme, moderate, absent), for example, afraid of the dark when in bed at night, a little uneasy without a light, not at all afraid of the dark.
2   Fifteen items in which the parent had to record an impression of the frequency of certain kinds of behaviour (for instance, crying, nail-biting, headaches) on an eight-point scale ranging from 'never or less than once a year' to 'every day or nearly every day'.

The types of behaviour covered are shown in *Appendix 1* (pp. 155–57). They covered most of the behaviour problems described in the currently available works on child psychiatry as occurring in school-age children clinically assessed as being 'disturbed', 'maladjusted', and so on.

A few, more extreme, forms of behaviour described in clinic patients were *not* included. These were (i) the most bizarre forms of abnormal behaviour (for example, autism, hallucinations, obsessional behaviour); (ii) sexual problems, and (iii) certain kinds of blatantly delinquent behaviour, such as arson. Such types of behaviour appeared to be rare even among clinic patients in our age group and, therefore, we felt that the possible value of their inclusion in revealing 'undiagnosed' cases was much outweighed by the possibly adverse effects on response (and public goodwill) of including too many items relating specifically to what our informants might see as 'the mad and the bad'. Space was made available on the form, however, for them to outline anything not covered by our questions which caused them concern about the child. In general this was used to describe minor incidents, relating to the child's mannerisms, eating habits, lack of school progress, for example, or for expansion on items already underlined with only a very few more serious aberrations being recorded.

To facilitate analysis relating the children's behaviour at home to other aspects of their life, we felt it was also desirable to establish some overall index of behavioural deviation. Originally it was intended to use, for this purpose, each child's total problem score in terms of the total number of extreme items underlined by the parents. This wide score would have given each problem the same weight without regard to the frequency with which it occurred. Information gained in the survey about the distribution of each behaviour trait, however, showed clearly that some types of extreme behaviour were much more common than others. For example, about one in five of the girls of all ages whose parents provided information were said to be very faddy about what they ate. Where behaviour was reported so frequently it was felt that it would scarcely be justifiable to see it as contributing to an index of abnormality. Furthermore in the original survey, where we covered an eleven-year age range, it was felt that we should take some account of the changing incidence of a given type of behaviour at different ages. For instance *crying* more than once a week was extremely rare among fourteen-year-old boys, where only 1 per cent were affected, but quite common (25 per cent) among those aged six.

To allow for these factors, it was decided to adopt a concept of 'deviating' behaviour[2] framed in terms of a 10 per cent limit: that is only those types of behaviour, reported to have occurred at an

---

[2] In the original study, this is referred to as 'deviant' behaviour. Since then, however, the term 'deviant' has acquired connotations of social disapproval rather than statistical variation so, to avoid confusion, the number of items of atypical behaviour manifested by any individual will now be referred to as their 'deviation' score.

intensity or frequency found in 10 per cent or less of a given age and sex group, were considered to be a deviation for a child of that age and that sex. Thus, in the example given, crying more than once a week would be a deviation for the fourteen-year-old but not for the child of six. The overall deviation score for each person was then calculated by summing the number of items they were reported to manifest which were atypical for their particular age and their sex. As, in the present study, we are concerned with only one age-group, those aged nine at the time of the original survey, the calculation of the deviation score may seem superfluous. It was decided to continue to use it, however, in preference to a cruder problem score. One reason was to maintain continuity with the original study – another, perhaps more important, lay in the avoidance of subjective decisions about what did, or did not, constitute a 'problem' of behaviour.

The teacher's questionnaire covered data on attainment, attendance, and physical disabilities as well as the manifestation of behaviour problems in school (see *Appendix 2*, pp. 162–64). As no behavioural items occurred in more than 10 per cent of cases, an unadjusted 'total problem score' was used here.

Taken together, then, these two approaches produced comprehensive information about the performance, in the two main spheres of their lives, of a highly representative cross-section of 'normal' school-children in that particular area of south-east England.[3] As such they seemed to provide a useful basis for studying the relationship, if any, between childhood behaviour and subsequent life experiences.

COVERAGE FOR THE NEW STUDY

It would clearly be an impossible task, both administratively and financially, to follow up the whole of the original 1961 sample (amounting to about 6,500 people). A decision had to be made,

---

[3] For full details of this study see Shepherd, M., Oppenheim, A. N., and Mitchell, S. (1971) *Childhood Behaviour and Mental Health*. London: University of London Press.

therefore, as to how we could limit numbers for the new study while still maintaining representativeness and also ensuring that we included enough cases of those who had shown atypical behaviour in childhood/adolescence to allow for subsequent analysis. Three possible solutions were considered.

First, a random sample of appropriate size could be drawn from the original group. This would certainly fulfil the criterion of representativeness. On the other hand the wide age range covered (eleven years) could cause considerable difficulties in later analysis. How, for example, could we find ways of equating the work history (in terms of number of jobs held, promotions, and so on) of those who were only twenty-two (the original five-year-olds) with those who were ten years older? Similar difficulties could be foreseen with respect to most aspects of life – health problems and matrimonial breakdown, for example, might be expected to be more prevalent among the older age groups. Furthermore, the environment itself, in terms of educational opportunity, work experience, family organization, and social mores, might well have caused differences to appear at the extremes between the experiences of those educated in the 1950s who entered adulthood in the 1960s and those who followed ten years later after a period of some social change. Clearly this problem was not insurmountable. It could have been met by subdividing the sample into smaller age-groups for analysis. This would, however, have also reduced the number of people in each age range and so contravened our second criterion, that is that there must be enough cases to allow for some representation of relatively rare forms of behaviour.

Second, we could meet this difficulty by trying to ensure that we included in the follow-up all those children whose behaviour in childhood had been most problematic. Such a group, consisting of the 10 per cent reported as most atypical by their parents, had already been established in the original survey, together with a group of controls (each individually matched to a deviator on grounds of sex, age, area of residence, and school) whose reported behaviour showed little or no deviation from the norm. These groups also presented the advantage that they had been re-surveyed in 1964, when parents and teachers had been asked to answer the same questions as in 1961, thereby producing information on short-term persistence of behavioural traits. They did, however, have two fairly major disadvantages. First, we were still left with the problem of a very wide age range with very small cell frequencies. Combination of different ages would present considerable difficulties not only in terms of the difficulty in reconciling experiences over different stages of the lifespan (already discussed) but also in terms of assessing the predictive value of specific types of behaviour in childhood. Qualitatively the same type of reported behaviour (for instance frequency of crying) could have very different connotations at different ages. Second, there was our criterion of representativeness. If we included only the deviators and their controls, we would be looking at extremes. Furthermore, though the 'deviators' might be seen as representative of children perceived as problematic by their parents (that is they constituted all the most atypical 10 per cent of children whose *parents completed forms* in 1961) the 'controls' were in no way representative of other 'normal' children. They had each been chosen deliberately as a good match for a specific deviator. Furthermore, by concentrating on deviators and controls we would also omit a large part of the original sample made up of those children who were neither completely problem-free nor in the 'worst' 10 per cent. As 10 per cent was a purely arbitrary cut-off point, this would seem unfortunate. If we were to be able to establish any link between reported childhood behaviour and later experiences then surely we must have information about children who conformed to, or deviated from, the norm for their age to differing extents and in different ways – we wanted as many different types of children as possible.

The third possibility, then, was to think of ways of maximizing representativeness in terms of range of behaviour even though this entailed cutting back on representativeness in other ways. Instead of trying to cover the *whole* of the original sample, we could limit ourselves to specific age groups and then follow up *all* the children from the original sample (including those 7 per cent whose parents had not filled in their questionnaires) who fell into the appropriate category. We would then not only be able to relate childhood behaviour to later life, but also be in a position to find out what happened to a representative sample of children who in 1961 were aged X years and attending local authority schools in Buckinghamshire.

In adopting this approach, we had to think hard and long about which age groups to include. The right choices were not obvious since points could be made for and against all age groups. There appeared, however, to be two main criteria which must be considered. First, we should *avoid any age group where coverage might be incomplete*. This excluded the fifteen-year-olds since the original survey (carried out during the summer term) excluded all those who had already left school at Christmas or Easter and over-represented those who were voluntarily staying on to get academic qualifications. Secondly, we decided to *exclude those age groups who had been subject to particularly stressful educational situations* in 1961. Two groups were seen as at risk – five-year-olds starting school and those aged from ten to twelve who were, first, involved in the strain of the eleven-plus procedures of selection for different types of secondary education and, subsequently, the actual move to their new school. Selection of one of these age groups would certainly have provided information about those who reacted adversely to stress. It would also tend to increase the number of cases of transitory behaviour problems associated with specific, immediate structural factors and once again it was believed (perhaps wrongly with hindsight) that this could cause difficulties with interpretation and analysis at a later stage.

So far as the remaining groups were concerned, the final choice was arbitrary. The fourteen-year-olds were selected to represent adolescents, the nine-year-olds as a pre-pubertal group. Both groups were studied but it is only the former nine-year-olds who will be discussed in the present book.

PREPARATION OF INTERVIEW SCHEDULE

The number and types of questions which could be asked in an investigation of this kind are clearly almost limitless. Any attempt to devise a small number of questions which can reveal the nature of different individuals' experiences, subjective and objective, over a sixteen-year period can provide only a very patchy and incomplete picture. Each person's life is so individual and multi-faceted that we could attempt to relate childhood behaviour to subsequent outcome only in the crudest of terms. The schedule, then, was designed with the following criteria in mind.

1   It should include items which would provide objective information about each individual's history since 1961 and also more subjective information about how they saw their lives.
2   The schedules were to be administered by a number of relatively unskilled interviewers. The format, therefore, should be such as to cut down the degree of interviewer spontaneity, interpretation, and so on.
3   In deciding which aspects of a person's life we should investigate and how deeply we should do so, we once again had to attempt to balance the desirability of covering problem areas (for example, involvement in deviant behaviour) and the equally important criterion that we should avoid causing offence to interviewees. This latter proviso not only was important from an ethical viewpoint, but also could be a source of 'public relations' problems (such as letters to the local papers and consequent refusals to be interviewed).

The schedule which was designed is attached as *Appendix 3* (pp. 165–77). It includes coverage of the main aspects of each individual's biography since 1961 – school, work, marriage relationships, housing, health, involvement in court proceedings – together with some assessments, made by the individuals themselves, of the 'quality' of their life.

In the first draft of the questionnaire other topics were included – questions on political and religious affiliations and involvement, and much more detailed questions concerning participation in criminal and deviant activities. These items were dropped after the piloting of the schedule in autumn 1977. The questions on religious beliefs or affiliations, somewhat to our astonishment, produced some hostility from those who *did* have such beliefs but felt that these were private. Questions on political affiliations and voting behaviour also produced some disquiet, some informants having to be reassured that such questions did not have ulterior motives and that we were not disguised canvassers. The detailed questions on criminal involvement, either as victim or as offender, strangely enough did *not* produce resentment, merely boredom as we went through our list of possible deviations, none of which applied!

As a result of this pilot exercise we therefore decided to abandon the questions on religion and politics (though this was subsequently regretted) and to cut down the questions on criminal involvement into the more concentrated, if less illuminating, form shown in Section G. of the schedule.

APPOINTMENT AND INDUCTION OF INTERVIEWERS

Advertisements for part-time interviewers were placed in local newspapers in autumn 1977. Each applicant was asked to provide references of good character and such references were all checked. All candidates were also interviewed in their homes by the principal investigator and research assistant. By December 1977 we had appointed twenty-two suitable interviewers and briefing sessions were held at four local centres. At these sessions, each lasting about three hours, the interviewers were introduced to the schedule and provided with written notes relating to its administration and possible problems of interpretation. Each person had also to carry out a trial interview where the interviewer (either one of the research staff or another trainee interviewer) had been provided with a script introducing problematic responses. This we found a very useful exercise, as did the interviewers themselves, as it provided clear, first-hand experience of the inaccuracies they could perpetrate if they interviewed too casually.

The interviewers then carried out one genuine interview, which was immediately returned to us for checking, and thereafter submitted their completed schedules weekly together with a detailed worksheet which acted both as the basis for calculating their pay and also as our source of information on how each case was progressing.

The five additional interviewers employed later, as replacements, were briefed in a similar manner.

TRACING

The first step in autumn 1977 was to consult the current electoral rolls for the relevant areas. In this way it was possible to ascertain whether the potential respondent or anyone of the same surname still lived at the old address or, because of possible postal changes or inaccuracies in recording, in the relevant street. This method provided leads for about 40 per cent of our sample. Clearly, however, a great deal still remained to be done by other methods. In particular it became apparent that our interviewers (calling at addresses near those where missing respondents had lived) would be well placed to conduct on-the-spot enquiries. This, however, presented some difficulties. The people we had engaged had been selected as *interviewers* not tracers and while some were enthusiastic detectives, others clearly felt far from comfortable making enquiries from neighbours, and considerable ingenuity and perseverance were often required to bring a search to a successful conclusion. For example, in one case where the family had left the area some years before, our fieldworker contacted four sets of neighbours (with no results), tried the local shop unsuccessfully but at their suggestion contacted a retired postman who, in turn, mentioned that an ex-neighbour was now living in a nearby old people's home, and she was finally able to direct us to a mutual friend who did have the parents' new address. We wrote to them and so the respondent's current address was obtained.

The ability to recruit and maintain a staff of fieldworkers with the right characteristics is clearly very important in enquiries of this type. We found, however, that this presented considerable problems. The supply of suitable people was limited since this was an area of high employment with no shortage of *permanent* full- and part-time jobs. Most of our fieldworkers were limited in the amount of time they could devote to the survey either because of domestic commitments or because they were already in full-time employment. There was also a fairly high level of attrition as our people found permanent jobs, cleared their debts, moved house, had babies, and so on. It therefore became apparent that supplementary methods of tracing must be tried – for example, the use of telephone directories in the town or area where the respondent or his/her parents were known to be living. Likely prospects were then contacted by telephone so that we could check whether or not they were the right people. This method proved quite successful in the case of people with uncommon surnames or those who lived in small towns or villages but trying to find the Jones family in Cardiff or the MacDonalds in Glasgow presented difficulties. The possibility of using marriage registers was also explored since this would provide a married name for girls plus details of both sets of parents. A trial run at St Catherine's House, London, did produce results but it proved an extremely arduous and time-consuming process. It was also expensive, as the data we required were revealed only by buying the relevant marriage certificates, and consequently was abandoned after a two-day trial run. Other approaches, for instance to local authority housing departments, also proved of very limited assistance because of the demands of confidentiality. Thus while they might agree to pass on letters from us to present tenants, they would not disclose addresses or even areas of those who had moved.

The final method of tracing was used only when it became apparent that the success of our own on-the-spot efforts had come to an end, leaving a number of people untraced. We applied to the Ethical Committee of the Central Statistical Office for permission to use the tracing facilities of the National Health Service Central Registry at Southport which should, we thought, be able to give us 100 per cent coverage. Again, however, ethical considerations made the use of this resource somewhat cumbersome. Because of the need for confidentiality, the Central Registry could provide us only with the NHS number of the person we asked about, together with the name of the Area Health Authority where his current registration was recorded. We then wrote to that Area Health Authority asking if they would tell us the name and address of the doctor with whom this person was registered (enclosing a prepaid reply envelope and form). When this was returned, we then contacted the doctor concerned asking for permission to approach the patient (again enclosing a prepaid postcard with a statement of consent which the GP just had to sign and return). The doctor's consent was sent back to the Area Health Authority who were then enabled to forward a communication from us to the potential respondent. We were at no time provided with the person's address and had no way of knowing whether or not our communications had reached them.

TRACING EFFECTIVENESS

As a result of these various techniques we succeeded in tracing and contacting, directly or indirectly, all but twenty-five of the original nine-year-old girls and twenty-two of the boys. Of these, four males and one female were known to have died; the rest could not be traced at all even through the health registration data. The reasons for this were twofold. About two-thirds of the losses occurred because the names we had were not traceable by the health authorities as either they had left the care of the health service (through emigration or 'going private' for example) or their existence had never been officially recorded. This second group included one or two people who may never have registered for medical treatment (for example, children of American servicemen) but, in the main, probably involved cases where the individual's name as recorded by us in 1961 did not conform exactly to that recorded by the health service. The other main source of difficulty lay not so much in failure to trace as in failure to contact – that is, where either the Area Health Authority or the family doctors were not prepared to cooperate or a few cases where the individual concerned had moved from the address recorded.

POSTAL APPROACH

Our original intention was to obtain all our information by interview. It rapidly became apparent, however, that this was going to present enormous practical difficulties. There were two main interrelated problems. First, the geographical dispersion of our 1961 sample group meant that we had addresses ranging from Aberdeen to Cornwall inside Britain and many worldwide. Secondly, we wanted to control as much as possible the effects of different interviewers. If we were to try to interview all our potential respondents (or more realistically, those still in mainland Britain) we were faced with two choices. We would either have to find interviewers in the areas where these people lived or we should have to send interviewers the length and breadth of the country from a central pool. Both alternatives presented considerable problems. Dispatching our own interviewers round the country would have been extremely costly even if our (very much part-time) interviewers had been willing to contemplate such journeys. Our experiences in the local area showed that a single visit did not always result in a successful interview. Even when advance notice was given the interviewer might find that the person to be interviewed was busy, had visitors, had gone out, or for some other reason, the appointment had to be postponed (sometimes more than once). Sending an interviewer to a distant area and keeping her/him there for possibly several days to achieve one or two interviews would have been prohibitively expensive. Using multiple local interviewers, each carrying out one or two interviews, appeared to offer little advantage (in terms of standardization of approach, establishing contact, and so on) over using our potential respondents to interview themselves – that is, sending them a suitably modified postal questionnaire.

This possibility was explored by sending a modified version of the interviewer's schedule to a small number (twelve) of people of varying social and educational background who were not part of the follow-up group but whose addresses, outside Buckingham-shire, had been obtained in the course of earlier pilot stages. Scrutiny of the eleven questionnaires returned indicated that respondents were able to understand the questionnaire and that the data provided was, if anything, rather more detailed than that recorded by interviewers.

As will be seen in a subsequent section, the use of postal questionnaires resulted in a reduced response rate compared with an approach by an interviewer. It did, however, enable us to get some responses from people living or working overseas who would otherwise have been quite inaccessible (for example, one young man who was hitch-hiking round the world and who, with the help of his mother, we finally contacted 'c/o Poste Restante, Athens'). A second benefit, admittedly unforeseen when we originally decided to supplement interviews with postal question-naires, was that this enabled us, later, to contact people traced through the assistance of the NHS Central Registry. Finally (though this applied to only a few people) it was possible to use the postal questionnaire to re-approach (often successfully) people who did not wish to be interviewed or whose parents refused to divulge their whereabouts.

RESPONSE

By the time fieldwork finished at the beginning of 1978, we had received information by interview or postal questionnaire from 81 per cent of the women and 78 per cent of the men whom we had been able to trace and who were still alive. This overall figure, however, conceals the considerable variation in success which occurred between our different methods of approach. Of those visited by an interviewer (160 females, 170 males), only 10 women and 7 men refused to cooperate (that is 95 per cent success); among those sent postal questionnaires, the response rate fell to 61 per cent. Again, however, the total postal return data may be misleading. Where we approached the person *directly* using an address (including those abroad) obtained through our own efforts, nearly three-quarters of those concerned sent back completed questionnaires: where the letters and forms were forwarded through health service channels this fell to only one in three of those who had apparently been contacted.

These figures obviously provide support for the argument that a direct person-to-person approach is the best basis for a high response rate. It is necessary, however, to qualify this slightly since included in the postal approach are some cases that might otherwise have become interview 'failures' – for example, people who were never at home (despite repeated calls, use of appointment letters, and so on) and people whose parents denied access to them (but who apparently forwarded mail since the questionnaire was returned completed in half these cases). Where this second approach was also unsuccessful, the case has appeared as a 'postal' failure and not as an 'interviewer' one. A second point about the *direct* postal approach is that it included those potential respondents who currently lived overseas and, from these, only 60 per cent of questionnaires were returned. We have treated the others as non-respondents but it may well be that some of them never received their questionnaires and should really be classified as not traced.

The main difference in postal response, however, clearly lies between those approached directly by us and those where the envelope (containing our letter, the questionnaire, and the return envelope) was addressed and forwarded by the local health authority offices. Unfortunately the reason for the marked drop in response is impossible to determine. It may lie in the characteristics of the potential respondents themselves and be connected with our difficulty in tracing them; it may reflect the fact that those traced by our own efforts would have been more likely to hear of us before receiving the questionnaire (for example, from the parents or neighbours who provided their address); it may be a result of the method of forwarding the questionnaire; or, indeed, it may have involved a combination of all three.

POSSIBLE BIAS

Our total losses, taking together those we could not contact and those who were unwilling to provide information, amounted to 26 per cent of the original group of nine-year-olds. This is quite a substantial proportion making it necessary to ask to what extent our non-respondents may have differed from those we were able to contact and who did cooperate. This is always a difficult question to answer but the availability of the original (1961) information at least made it possible to compare the characteristics in childhood of respondents and non-respondents. This revealed only minimal differences. Looking first at behaviour, it was quite obvious that the respondents had been no 'better' as children: 11 per cent of each sex had a deviation score of four or more as nine-year-olds (that is they conform to the norms of the 1961 group as a whole). The distribution of particular types of extreme behaviour was also practically identical with that found for all nine-year-olds in 1961. In fact, the only differences of more than 1 per cent occurring were, *for the girls*, food fads (17 per cent of respondents in 1978 compared with 21 per cent in 1961); small appetites (10 per cent and 13 per cent respectively); irritability (10 per cent and 12 per cent); and lying (1 per cent and 3 per cent). *Among the boys*, those with reading difficulties at nine were slightly underrepresented in the follow-up (21 per cent and 25 per cent) as, to a very minor extent, were those who had been irritable (10 per cent and 12 per cent) and those who had been faddy about food (20 per cent and

22 per cent). Conversely those who had been afraid of the dark were slightly overrepresented (12 per cent compared with 10 per cent for all nine-year-old boys).

There was no evidence, therefore, that those we could not contact, or who refused to cooperate, in 1978 had started out with any excess of psychological problems in 1961. Nor did they appear to differ with respect to social criteria. Analysis of response rates in terms of the socio-economic category (Hall Jones Scale) of the *fathers'* jobs in 1961 showed that response remained constant at between 74 and 78 per cent in six out of the nine possible occupational categories. The exceptions were the particularly *high* rate of responses (86 per cent) among those whose fathers were then in *unskilled manual* jobs and, conversely, a *lower* rate (61 per cent) among those whose fathers occupied managerial or executive positions and those whose fathers were unemployed, sick, dead, missing, and so on in 1961 (also 61 per cent response). If bias exists among our respondents, then, it appears that it occurs at both ends of the continuum of social privilege.

ANALYSIS AND PRESENTATION

Analysis was carried out using the VAX computer of the University of Stirling and involved the generation of very much more material than is being presented here. Many cross-tabulations showed no relationship between the variables concerned. These have been included only where the lack of association is germane to the main line of argument being pursued – in particular, where there are *a priori* grounds for expecting that a relationship *would* exist. This might be seen as so reasonable as not to require comment. There is, however, one subgroup of omissions which does call for further expansion – those which pertain to the relationship between childhood behaviour and subsequent events. Since the purpose of the study was to consider this relationship, considerable time and effort was devoted to appropriate analysis. That concerned with the total deviation score of our informants at the age of nine presented little difficulty.

The main problem concerned the individual behaviour traits and was twofold. In the first place, the number of people showing some particular types of behaviour (for example, truancy or fear of strangers) at nine were very small. The second difficulty lay in the lack of cohesiveness between these individual traits. Clearly if there are not enough cases to make possible analysis in terms of discrete categories, one may fare better by grouping together various categories which seem to have some similarity or which appear to reflect some underlying common theme. This can be done on the basis of the researcher's own 'knowledge' (for example, 'let's push all the different types of "fear" into one group!') but, preferably, is accomplished by statistical examination of patterns emerging from the data. Our attempts to find such patterns, using every technique available on the computer, were entirely fruitless. Although disappointing this was not altogether unexpected in view of similar difficulties experienced at the time of the original survey. It has led, however, to the absence of reportable data concerning types of behaviour. Where the analysis showed some association of behaviour type with what occurred subsequently, this has, of course, been recorded. Where, however, the analysis has revealed no association (as indeed where the number of cases was too small to allow meaningful analysis) detailed figures have not been cited.

A further omission which may be noted by readers relates to the attribution of statistical significance to findings. This convention of statistical presentation, we feel, not only is distracting for the reader but also, particularly for the statistically naive person, can convey a misleading impression that some figures are more meaningful than others.

Statistical significance refers to the probability of differences, observed between groups, occurring by chance. If the probability is very low then we can assume that the groups are in fact different and not just showing slight variation from a common norm. The calculations to establish such probability depend, of course, on the size of the difference between groups in terms of relative occurrence of the attribute being studied *but* they also take into account the size of the groups concerned. If the groups are large, quite small differences may be significant; conversely if they are small, large observed differences may still have a relatively high probability of occurring by chance. This should be borne in mind by non-statistical readers when they are assessing findings. It may be, however, that several differences though individually non-significant may *together* present a consistent picture of more importance than several unrelated items which are significant.

One further convention which we have flouted is that of presenting a review of the literature and relating all findings to previous work. In the present case the choice of which literature to include was difficult since, while there was little of direct relevance, there was a great deal which could have been quoted in specific areas. Longitudinal studies following people from childhood into adult life are few. Cross-sectional studies pertaining to topics raised here – educational opportunity, for example – on the other hand, are very numerous indeed. There are also theoretical and methodological issues – for example, those relating to the classification of socio-economic status groups which form a vast field of study in their own right. To attempt to do justice to all such partially relevant work would have greatly increased the size of this book without necessarily adding to the understanding of the general reader. We have therefore decided to withhold *all* reference to the work of others.

— 2

EDUCATION

In 1961 the sample were nine years old and all attending local authority primary schools. There was nevertheless variation in type of school in terms of size and organization so that, while 40 per cent of the children attended relatively small schools, where all the children of one age group (or even more than one) could be accommodated in a single class, the other 60 per cent found themselves in large schools where some form of 'streaming' was adopted within a single age cohort. Here the usual system of allocation adopted was one of 'merit', that is based on some measure of classroom attainment, which accounted for three out of four children in a streamed environment and nearly half (45 per cent) of the whole sample. Relatively few (10 per cent) of children attended schools where the age group was divided into equal groups on the base of some neutral criterion such as month of birth or first letter of surname. Of the children attending two-stream schools, as might be expected about half (52 per cent) were in the top stream (with a better performance among girls where 58 per cent were in the top class compared to only 48 per cent of boys). Of those attending schools divided into three or more merit streams (18 per cent of the sample) rather more than expected (42 per cent) were in the top stream, rather fewer (17 per cent) in the bottom.

Teachers' assessments of the children as a whole (including those in unstreamed schools) were rather less favourable with 30 per cent rated as 'below average' for age and type of school and only 20 per cent as 'above average'. This was particularly marked in the case of the boys where 36 per cent were seen as 'below average' compared with only 24 per cent of girls. Sex differences were also marked in teachers' assessments of reading ability as 32 per cent (one in three) of boys were rated as 'below average' readers compared to only 20 per cent (one in five) of the girls.

TYPE OF SECONDARY SCHOOL

In 1962–63 these children met the hurdle of the dreaded 'eleven-plus' selection process which was still operating in the area. As *Table 1* shows about a third of the boys and about a quarter of the girls went to a selective school (that is grammar or technical) either at eleven or, in a few cases, by late transfer at thirteen; a very small proportion were taken out of the state educational system and sent to private schools; and the rest (two-thirds of the

Table 1 *Type of secondary school attended by sex*

	type of secondary school attended			
	grammar	*technical*	*non-selective*	*private*
boys	60 (24.4)	21 (8.5)	162 (65.9)	3 (1.2)
girls	50 (21.1)	7 (2.9)	176 (73.9)	5 (2.1)

boys, three-quarters of the girls) continued their education at a secondary modern school or, in one area, a comprehensive (but as considerable 'creaming' took place by the local grammar and technical schools, this has been classed as basically secondary modern). The three children attending special schools have also been placed in this 'non-selective' group.

RELATIONSHIP BETWEEN PRIMARY SCHOOL AND
SECONDARY EDUCATION

To what extent was it possible to predict secondary school opportunities from an examination of each child's educational 'profile' at nine years of age?

First, the organizational pattern of the primary school attended did not, in itself, appear to affect a child's opportunity of attending a selective secondary school: 72 per cent of those attending schools with merit streaming went to non-selective schools, as did 67 per cent of those attending schools with no merit streaming. There was no difference between schools with only two merit-based streams and those with more. This broad picture, however, conceals a difference between the sexes. As *Table 2* shows, *boys* attending larger merit-streamed schools had an increased chance of going to selective type schools (40 per cent) whereas *girls* at such schools had the *lowest* success rate (20 per cent). How can this be explained? Were there perhaps more boys in the *top* stream of such larger schools? In fact, the reverse was marginally true with 9 per cent of the girls compared with 7 per cent of boys. Yet

Table 2   *Proportions of children proceeding to grammar, technical or private schools by type of primary school (in rank order)*

boys	merit-streamed school with 3+ streams	=	39.5%
boys	unstreamed/parallel-streamed schools	=	34.5%
boys	merit-streamed schools with 2 streams	=	31.7%
girls	unstreamed/parallel-streamed schools	=	30.5%
girls	merit-streamed schools with 2 streams	=	23.8%
girls	merit-streamed school with 3+ streams	=	20.3%

of these boys in the top stream of larger schools, only 19 per cent went to non-selective schools while of their female classmates more than half (57 per cent) did so.

Secondly, in general the teacher's assessment of the *child's* normal *place in class* at the age of nine years appears a good predictor of type of secondary school. *Table 3* shows clearly how little chance a child in the bottom 25 per cent of his/her teaching group at nine years old had of achieving a place in any but a non-selective secondary school. In the top quartile however, one in two of the girls and two out of three of the boys had a chance of the type of education which would open up further opportunities in terms of higher qualifications, for instance. Sex differences are still evident in the proportions of the 'best' academic nine-year-olds going on to selective schools and also in the increased likelihood of even 'middling' boys moving away from the non-selective sector. In part this seems due to the higher proportion of boys achieving places in technical schools (nearly three times as great as among the girls) but the boys also succeeded in getting a higher number of grammar school places.

Thirdly, can the difference be explained in terms of two of the attributes contributing to 'success' in eleven-plus assessment, that

Table 3 *Child's place in teaching group at nine years by type of secondary school attended*

type of secondary school	child in top 25%		child in middle 50% or variation with subject		child in bottom 25%	
	boys	girls	boys	girls	boys	girls
non-selective	27	35	68	83	61	49
	(34.6)	(47.9)	(69.4)	(80.6)	(95.3)	(94.2)
grammar, etc.	40	35	22	16	1	3
	(51.3)	(47.9)	(22.4)	(15.5)	(1.6)	(5.8)
technical	11	3	8	4	2	–
	(14.1)	(4.1)	(8.2)	(3.9)	(3.1)	(–)

Note: Totals for each school type may differ from those in Table 1, which includes pupils whose original attainment was not known.

is '*intelligence*' and *reading ability*? Although we obtained information about the results of standardized tests administered by
schools before the time of the first survey (1961) these unfortunately did not provide a basis for comparing all the children.
Some had not been tested at all and, where tests were used, they
were not always comparable. Some schools, for example, might
give an IQ based on a *verbal* test (involving also a degree of
literacy) while others used non-verbal ones (that is, where the
child completed designs and manipulated shapes).

Class teachers were asked also to assess each child's 'general
attainment' and 'reading ability' in relation to others of the same
age. This assessment will obviously include a stronger subjective
element than would the results of the 'objective tests'. Nevertheless, in the classroom-setting (and, particularly, in that of the
primary school where the class teacher tends to spend most of the
teaching day with a single class) it is the class teacher's subjective
assessment which carries most weight in terms of 'success', or lack
of it, for the child.

Table 4 shows that the best prediction of educational outcome
was to be rated 'below average' in reading ability or general attainment by one's teacher at the age of nine, particularly if one was a

Table 4   *Secondary school attended by teacher's assessment of the child at age nine*

		secondary school attended			
		non-selective		technical/grammar/private	
		boys	girls	boys	girls
reading ability	above average	24 (31.2)	42 (53.2)	53 (68.8)	37 (46.8)
at age nine	average	57 (67.9)	81 (79.5)	27 (32.1)	21 (20.5)
	below average	76 (97.4)	47 (95.9)	2 (2.6)	2 (4.1)
general attainment	above average	9 (18.8)	15 (31.3)	39 (81.3)	33 (68.8)
at age nine	average	62 (61.4)	99 (79.8)	39 (38.6)	25 (20.2)
	below average	85 (96.6)	52 (91.2)	3 (3.4)	5 (8.8)

boy. Being rated as 'above average' carried less certainty – particularly for girls. Thus of boys 'above average' in general attainment, only one in five finished up at a non-selective school but, among the girls, nearly a third did so. The situation was even more marked among those seen by their teachers as being of 'average' attainment where 80 per cent of girls went to a secondary modern type of school compared with only 61 per cent of similar boys.

Good reading ability at nine was a less reliable predictor than was the teacher's assessment of general attainment since more than half the girls of 'above average' reading ability found themselves at non-selective schools as did a third of the boys.

Absence from school (in nearly all cases because of illness) did not appear to have much association with type of secondary school. Among the boys, for example, two-thirds of those with minimal absences finished up at non-selective schools and so did two-thirds of those who had missed more than two weeks of schooling in their last completed term before the 1961 survey. Among the girls more of a trend was visible varying from 71 per cent of the best attenders to 79 per cent of the worst. Differences were small, however, and this is perhaps not surprising since absence in one particular term may well reflect a particular instance of ill-health rather than a pattern of absence perpetuated throughout the child's school career.

Fourthly, the manifestation of *behaviour problems in the classroom* at nine, however, did relate to 'success' at eleven. In 1961

Table 5 *Number of behaviour problems reported by teachers in 1961 by types of secondary school attended*

type of school	no problems		1 or 2		3 or more	
	boys	girls	boys	girls	boys	girls
non-selective	66 (54.5)	90 (68.7)	73 (73.0)	69 (77.5)	21 (87.5)	15 (88.2)
grammar	39 (32.2)	37 (28.2)	23 (23.0)	19 (21.3)	2 (8.3)	– (–)
technical	16 (13.2)	4 (3.1)	4 (4.0)	1 (1.1)	1 (4.2)	2 (11.8)

teachers were asked to indicate if the child concerned had manifested any of a selection of behaviour 'problems' covering a wide range of behaviour ranging from indications of personal malaise (for example, being 'withdrawn' or 'frightened') to more overt classroom misbehaviour. As *Table 5* shows, among both boys and girls, the children seen as most 'normal' and problem-free by their teachers were the most likely to be the academic successes, those with the most problems were the least likely to be selected for the more prestigious types of schools.

Before speculating about the deleterious effects of adverse classroom behaviour *per se*, however, it would be as well to

Table 6 *Recruitment to non-selective secondary school by educational level and classroom 'problem' rating at nine years*

attainment at nine years		boys number of classroom problems at nine years			girls number of classroom problems at nine years		
		none	1	2 or more	none	1	2 or more
above average	cell total no. (% of	31	12	5	33	11	4
	cell total) at non-selective secondary schools	5 (16.1)	4 (33.3)	nil (−)	12 (36.4)	2 (18.2)	1 (25.0)
average	cell total no. (% of	54	28	19	74	33	17
	cell total) at non-selective secondary schools	28 (51.9)	21 (75.0)	13 (68.4)	57 (77.0)	27 (81.8)	15 (88.2)
below average	cell total no. (% of	31	31	26	24	22	17
	cell total) at non-selective secondary schools	31 (100.0)	29 (93.5)	25 (96.2)	18 (75.0)	20 (90.9)	14 (82.4)

consider the relationship in 1961 between behaviour and general attainment. That there *is* a close relationship is clear when we compare the 'cell totals' in *Table 6*. Here we can see that, in each sex, the problem-free children present an approximately normal distribution in terms of attainment, that is one-quarter above average, half average, and about a quarter below average. When we look at those with problems, however, it becomes evident that the proportion of children in the above average category is falling while the proportion below average is rising. Thus among the boys, while the odds on being above to below average are equal for the problem-free, among those with a single problem they have decreased to 1:2.5, and among those with multiple problems to 1:5. Similar differences can be seen among the girls.

Since the two variables are so interrelated we must try to see how each operates if the other is held constant as in *Table 6*. Here we can see if we compare children with equal attributes, in terms of problems, that, in each case, those of above average attainment were much less likely to be recruited to non-selective schools than those with lower attainment. If we look only at the above average category on the other hand we cannot see any trend showing that number of problems has had a marked determining effect on the type of secondary school the child attended. Thus children with higher attainment but multiple problems were less likely to be recruited to non-selective schools than those with no problem. Among children of above average attainment at primary school, then, behaviour problems appear to carry little scholastic penalty.

Among those of average attainment, on the other hand, being problem-free appears to carry some weight in the secondary school selection process – particularly among the boys where only half of the problem-free average attainers finished up at non-selective schools compared with more than two-thirds of those with problems. Among the girls differences were smaller but still showed a slight educational advantage for the problem-free average pupil and also for the problem-free below average girl.

HOME FACTORS AND SECONDARY SCHOOL

Table 7 shows that the *occupational status of the child's father in 1961* bears some considerable relationship to later education. Thus we see that boys whose fathers were in 'higher' non-manual categories (that is had professional qualifications and/or were involved in higher administrative, managerial, or executive jobs) were more than twice as likely to get a grammar school type of education as were those whose fathers were in more routine white-collar jobs or skilled manual trades. Among the sons of semi-skilled or unskilled manual workers opportunities fell still lower. Among the girls, the chance of receiving a grammar school type of education was about one in two for those with fathers in the most prestigious white-collar jobs but only one in four for daughters of

Table 7 *Fathers' occupational status in 1961 by sex and secondary school type*

type of school	fathers' occupational status			
	non-manual		manual	
	higher (1–3)	lower (4 and 5)	skilled (6)	other (7 and 8)
boys				
non-selective	18 (34.6)	28 (73.7)	53 (69.7)	50 (78.1)
grammar	28 (53.8)	8 (21.1)	16 (21.1)	10 (15.6)
technical	6 (11.5)	2 (5.3)	7 (9.2)	4 (6.3)
total	52 (100.0)	38 (100.0)	76 (100.0)	64 (100.0)
girls				
non-selective	30 (49.2)	26 (70.3)	52 (83.9)	47 (85.5)
grammar	28 (45.9)	10 (27.0)	8 (12.9)	7 (12.7)
technical	3 (4.9)	1 (2.7)	2 (3.2)	1 (1.8)
total	61 (100.0)	37 (100.0)	62 (100.0)	55 (100.0)

Table 8 *Relationship between child's attainment at primary school, father's socio-economic status and type of secondary school attended*

attainment at primary school	boys			girls		
	grammar	technical	non-selective	grammar	technical	non-selective
father in professional, managerial, or executive job (higher level)						
above average	18 (100.0)	– (–)	– (–)	15 (78.9)	– (–)	4 (21.1)
average	8 (36.4)	6 (27.3)	8 (36.4)	8 (28.6)	3 (10.7)	17 (60.7)
below average	2 (18.2)	– (–)	9 (81.8)	5 (41.7)	– (–)	7 (58.3)
father in routine or minor supervisory white-collar job						
above average	3 (60.0)	1 (20.0)	1 (20.0)	5 (62.5)	– (–)	3 (37.5)
average	4 (25.0)	1 (6.3)	11 (68.8)	5 (20.8)	1 (4.2)	18 (75.0)
below average	– (–)	– (–)	15 (100.0)	– (–)	– (–)	2 (100.0)
father in skilled manual job						
above average	10 (58.8)	2 (11.8)	5 (29.4)	6 (54.5)	– (–)	5 (45.5)
average	5 (19.2)	3 (11.5)	18 (69.2)	2 (6.9)	2 (6.9)	25 (86.2)
below average	– (–)	– (–)	28 (100.0)	– (–)	– (–)	19 (100.0)
father in semi-skilled or unskilled job						
above average	5 (62.5)	– (–)	3 (37.5)	5 (62.5)	1 (12.5)	2 (25.0)
average	5 (15.6)	4 (12.5)	23 (71.9)	2 (6.25)	– (–)	30 (93.8)
below average	– (–)	– (–)	23 (100.0)	– (–)	– (–)	15 (100.0)
father's job not known, no father, father not working						
above average	– (–)	– (–)	– (–)	1 (50.0)	– (–)	1 (50.0)
average	2 (40.0)	1 (20.0)	2 (40.0)	2 (18.2)	– (–)	9 (81.8)
below average	– (–)	1 (9.1)	10 (90.9)	– (–)	– (–)	9 (100.0)

Note: Differences in numbers between this table and the previous one are accounted for by those whose attainment at nine years was not known other non-manual workers and one in eight for *all* those whose fathers were in manual occupations. It is also remarkable that in both higher non-manual and skilled manual groups, the chances of girls going to non-selective schools are much higher than those of their male counterparts.

Again, however, it is necessary to consider how these findings relate to perceived attainment at nine years old. As *Table 8* shows, within each socio-economic status group attainment level is important with the likelihood of receiving a grammar-school type of education decreasing sharply as attainment drops when we compare the different socio-economic groups. However, it is evident that, for any level of attainment, those children with fathers in the highest status group were most likely to attend a grammar school and least likely to finish their secondary schooling in a secondary modern. It is also noticeable that children of *average* attainment in this group were more likely to achieve *technical* school places than were those in other status groups. It is interesting to note that for all status groups, except the semi/unskilled one, high attainment girls were more likely to attend non-selective schools than were their male counterparts.

The main purpose of the 1961 survey was to obtain information about *behaviour problems exhibited at home*. Deviation scores were compiled which recorded the number of behaviour traits manifested which were atypical for the child's age and sex. As *Table 9* shows the relationship between such deviant behaviour at home and school 'success' is not self-evident. Among the boys it is certainly true that those with the highest number of deviant traits

Table 9 *Behaviour at home at nine years by secondary school*

type of school	number of deviant traits (boys)				number of deviant traits (girls)			
	0	1	2 or 3	4+	0	1	2 or 3	4+
non-selective	60	37	32	22	78	38	28	15
	(59.4)	(67.3)	(61.5)	(84.6)	(71.6)	(76.0)	(73.7)	(62.5)
grammar	31	12	17	3	29	9	10	7
	(30.7)	(21.8)	(32.7)	(11.5)	(26.6)	(18.0)	(26.3)	(29.2)
technical	10	6	3	1	2	3	–	2
	(9.9)	(10.9)	(5.8)	(3.8)	(3.7)	(6.0)	(–)	(8.3)

(that is the 4+ group) were considerably less likely to attend selective schools later. This did not apply to the girls, however, where the most problematic were the *most* likely to succeed. It is also noteworthy that in each sex, those with two or three deviant items of behaviour differed very little from those with none in terms of secondary school attended.

If we control for attainment, does the situation become any clearer? *Table 10* shows that for those of *above average attainment*, the manifestation of deviant behaviour at home has little or no deleterious effect on secondary school selection. Indeed, in each sex, the small number of above average children with four or more deviant traits *all* got grammar school places. Perhaps more surprising is the very high proportion of problem-free or single-problem girls of above average attainment who finished up at non-selective schools. One can only speculate about possible causes. Were they the 'well-adjusted', 'feminine' little girls who saw their future as non-competitive/non-academic or did their adjustment give rise to a false picture of academic competence not borne out in the eleven-plus selection tests? Did they (or their parents) reject the educational system or were they rejected by it? We cannot give an answer from the data available, unfortunately.

Among both boys and girls of *average* attainment, number of deviant traits seems of little relevance to secondary school selection with the single exception of boys with a lot (four or more) of problems. The below average children predominantly landed up at non-selective schools regardless of presence, or number, of problems of behaviour.

AGE LEFT SCHOOL

Relatively few (30 per cent) of the group stayed on at school after the age of sixteen and 40 per cent left at fifteen, the first available legal opportunity. As *Table 11* shows, school leaving age was clearly related to the type of school attended so that those at grammar and technical schools were unlikely to leave before their

Table 10 *Relationship between type of secondary school attended, child's attainment at nine years and number of deviant traits manifested at home at nine years*

No. of deviant traits reported by parents	boys			girls		
	grammar	technical	non-selective	grammar	technical	non-selective
	attainment 'above average' at nine years					
none	19	1	6	14	–	10
	(73.1)	(3.8)	(23.1)	(58.3)	(–)	(41.7)
one	6	1	1	4	1	3
	(75.0)	(12.5)	(12.5)	(50.0)	(12.5)	(37.5)
two or three	9	1	2	7	–	1
	(75.0)	(8.3)	(16.7)	(87.5)	(–)	(12.5)
four or more	2	–	–	6	–	–
	(100.0)	(–)	(–)	(100.0)	(–)	(–)
	attainment 'average' at nine years					
none	9	8	24	13	2	45
	(22.0)	(19.5)	(58.4)	(21.7)	(3.3)	(75.0)
one	6	5	13	4	2	30
	(25.0)	(20.8)	(54.2)	(11.1)	(5.6)	(83.3)
two or three	7	2	14	2	–	13
	(30.4)	(8.7)	(60.9)	(13.3)	(–)	(86.7)
four or more	2	–	9	–	2	8
	(18.2)	(–)	(81.8)	(–)	(20.0)	(80.0)
	attainment 'below average' at nine years					
none	1	–	27	2	–	20
	(3.6)	(–)	(96.4)	(9.1)	(–)	(90.9)
one	–	–	23	1	–	5
	(–)	(–)	(100.0)	(16.7)	(–)	(83.3)
two or three	1	–	15	1	–	12
	(6.3)	(–)	(93.8)	(7.7)	(–)	(92.3)
four or more	–	1	12	1	–	7
	(–)	(7.7)	(92.3)	(12.5)	(–)	(87.5)

sixteenth birthday (and, indeed, for them such early leaving required special permission). More interesting, perhaps, is the relatively high proportion of pupils *at non-selective schools* who stayed on voluntarily, usually for a further year. When these 'late leavers' are examined in respect of their attainment at nine years

Table 11 *school leaving age by type of school*

type of school		age left school			
		15	16	17	18
boys	grammar	–	13	13	38
		(–)	(20.3)	(20.3)	(59.4)
	technical	1	7	4	9
		(4.8)	(33.3)	(19.0)	(42.9)
	non-selective	96	54	10	1
		(59.6)	(33.5)	(6.2)	(0.6)
girls	grammar	4	17	6	29
		(7.1)	(30.4)	(10.7)	(51.8)
	technical	1	–	3	3
		(14.3)	(–)	(42.9)	(42.9)
	non-selective	112	53	6	4
		(64.0)	(30.3)	(3.4)	(2.3)

of age we find that 78 per cent of above average boys at non-selective schools and 60 per cent of above average girls stayed on until they were at least sixteen. For the below average the figures had fallen to 34 per cent and 23 per cent respectively.

Among *grammar school* pupils the most able girls at primary school were inclined to leave rather earlier than the others in that a lower proportion stayed past their eighteenth birthday (47 per cent compared with 58 and 60 per cent respectively for the average and below average groups).

QUALIFICATIONS GAINED AT SCHOOL

Some type of qualification was gained at school by 54 per cent of boys and 52 per cent of girls. The earlier leaving age of girls, however, showed itself in a shortfall in the number of girls obtaining A-levels, particularly among those obtaining three or more passes (12 per cent of boys compared with only 6 per cent of girls). As might be expected, the picture also varied with type of school so that, while only three children at grammar or private schools (all girls) failed to gain a single qualification, this was true of 70 per cent of boys attending non-selective schools and 63 per cent of girls. *Table 12* gives a more detailed breakdown of the *type of qualifications* obtained and shows clearly that those attending non-selective schools only in rare cases obtained more than the CSE (Certificate of Secondary Education) qualifications or a few passes at O-level. Those attending grammar schools, on the other hand, seldom achieved fewer than four O-level passes and nearly half of them passed one or more subjects at the higher A-level. At A-level the technical school pupils also seemed to do well (as well as their grammar school contemporaries) but they were rather less successful in number of O-level passes.

How far could we have predicted secondary school 'success' (in terms of qualifications gained) from the original primary school teachers' assessments of attainment when the children were nine

Table 12 *Qualifications gained by type of school*

	number of passes gained						
	CSE		O-level			A-level	
	1–4	5+	1–3	4–7	8+	1–2	3+
boys							
grammar	9	–	5	31	28	11	23
(64)	(14.1)	(–)	(7.8)	(48.4)	(43.8)	(17.2)	(35.9)
technical	2	1	4	10	5	5	6
(21)	(9.5)	(4.8)	(19.0)	(47.6)	(23.8)	(23.8)	(28.6)
non-selective	15	27	14	9	4	1	1
(161)	(9.3)	(16.8)	(8.7)	(5.6)	(2.5)	(0.6)	(0.6)
girls							
grammar	4	–	7	22	24	15	13
(56)	(7.1)	(–)	(12.5)	(39.3)	(42.9)	(26.8)	(23.2)
technical	1	1	2	3	2	1	2
(7)	(14.3)	(14.3)	(28.6)	(42.9)	(28.6)	(14.3)	(28.6)
non-selective	18	33	22	12	–	5	–
(175)	(10.3)	(18.9)	(12.6)	(6.9)	(–)	(2.9)	(–)

years old? *Table 13* indicates that there is an association but that this is at its most marked (i) in the lack of qualifications gained by below average children and (ii) in predicting the widest range of possible qualifications (that is at least *one* O-level). Particularly worrying is the lack of success, relative to their male counterparts, of girls of above average and average attainment. Thus while nearly all the above average boys got at least one O-level, one in four of the equivalently ranked girls failed to do so.

Is this associated with the type of secondary school attended? It has already been shown (p. 28) that girls in the above average attainment group were more likely to attend non-selective schools and *Table 12* shows that pupils at such schools were less likely to gain O-level passes. *Table 14* indicates that this differential selection for secondary school may be important since acquisition of the minimal qualification of 'at least one O-level' by average or above average pupils does not manifest a sex difference when type of school is held constant. There is, however, a wide difference between the proportion of children of originally 'equal' attainment who gain a qualification at all. Thus while nearly all the pupils (whatever their primary school rating) who attended grammar or technical school achieved this minimal level only two

Table 13   *Secondary school qualifications by teacher's assessment at nine years and sex*

attainment	sex	qualifications gained		
		at least 1 O-level	8 or more O-levels	at least 1 A-level
above average	boys (N = 48)	43 (89.6)	21 (43.8)	26 (54.2)
	girls (N = 48)	37 (77.1)	14 (29.2)	15 (31.3)
average	boys (N = 99)	52 (52.5)	13 (13.1)	17 (17.3)
	girls (N = 124)	46 (37.1)	10 (8.1)	18 (14.5)
below average	boys (N = 88)	11 (12.5)	2 (2.3)	2 (2.3)
	girls (N = 57)	7 (12.3)	2 (3.5)	3 (5.3)

out of five of the 'above average' primary pupils who went to non-selective schools did so and less than a quarter of those seen as 'average' in 1961.

When we look at the top scores in O-level examinations (that is those with eight or more passes) and those with A-level qualifications, the above average girls at grammar school do less well than might be expected: the formerly average girls, on the other hand, do rather better than their male equals.

Table 14   *Qualifications gained at secondary school by teachers' assessment at nine years, types of secondary school attended and sex*

(percentages relate to per cent of attainment-group at kind of school)

attainment (1961)	type of school					
	grammar		technical		non-selective	
	boys	girls	boys	girls	boys	girls
gained at least 1 A-level						
above average	23	14	2	1	1	–
	(63.9)	(43.8)	(66.7)	(100.0)	(11.1)	(–)
average	9	11	7	2	1	5
	(37.5)	(57.9)	(46.7)	(33.3)	(1.6)	(5.1)
below average	1	3	1	no cases	–	–
	(50.0)	(60.0)	(100.0)	in group	(–)	(–)
gained 8 or more O-levels						
above average	18	14	2	–	1	–
	(50.0)	(43.8)	(66.7)	(–)	(11.1)	(–)
average	8	8	2	2	3	–
	(33.3)	(42.1)	(13.3)	(33.3)	(4.8)	(–)
below average	1	2	1	no cases	–	–
	(50.0)	(40.0)	(100.0)	in group	(–)	(–)
gained at least 1 O-level						
above average	36	30	3	1	4	6
	(100.0)	(93.7)	(100.0)	(100.0)	(44.4)	(40.0)
average	24	18	13	5	15	23
	(100.0)	(94.7)	(86.7)	(83.3)	(24.2)	(23.2)
below average	2	5	1	no cases	8	2
	(100.0)	(100.0)	(100.0)	in group	(9.4)	(3.8)

Table 15 *Type of educational or training course first attended (by last secondary school and sex)*

last secondary school attended	*type of course*				
	full-time academic	*full-time vocational*	*part-time job-related*	*'apprenticeship' training on the job but no college course*	*no formal training[1] or further education*
boys					
non-selective (N=160)	2 (1.3)	11 (6.9)	77 (48.1)	20 (12.5)	50 (31.3)
grammar (N=63)	23 (36.5)	12 (19.0)	23 (36.5)[1]	1 (1.6)	4 (6.3)
technical (N=21)	7 (33.3)	1 (4.8)	11 (52.4)	–(–)	2 (9.5)
all boys (N=244)[2]	32 (13.1)	24 (9.8)	111 (45.5)	21 (8.6)	56 (23.0)
girls					
non-selective (N=175)	4 (2.3)	20 (11.4)	52 (29.7)	18 (10.3)	81 (46.3)
grammar (N=56)	13 (23.2)	24 (42.9)	6 (10.7)	5 (8.9)	8 (14.3)
technical (N=7)	2 (28.6)	3 (42.9)	–(–)	–(–)	2 (28.6)
all girls (N=238)	19 (8.0)	47 (19.7)	58 (24.4)	23 (9.7)	91 (38.2)

Notes: [1] Included here are four males and four females who attended evening classes concerning purely leisure interest (all were from non-selective school).

[2] Excluded are two males where information on further education was lacking.

FURTHER EDUCATION AND TRAINING
AFTER SCHOOL

Most respondents said that they had enrolled in at least one further
education or college-based vocational training course after leaving
school though, as might be expected, grammar school pupils were
more likely to take advantage of such facilities than were those who
completed their education at non-selective schools. Full-time
academic education was almost entirely limited to those who had
attended grammar or technical schools (with about equal opportunities of so doing) and, though recruitment to full-time 'vocational' courses was more open, the chance of attending such a
course was still much reduced for the ex-secondary-modern pupil.
Indeed, the main source of further education for such pupils, of
either sex, lay in participation in part-time, that is evening and/or
job release courses. As *Table 15* shows, such opportunities were
taken up by nearly half the male non-selective school pupils but
only just over a quarter of the girls.

This sex difference was not limited to the non-selective school
pupils. As *Table 15* shows, for each school type the proportion of
girls saying they had taken no further education or formalized
training since leaving school was much higher than among the
equivalent boys. Sex differences also emerge in terms of the type
of course taken. Thus twice as many girls as boys enrolled in full-
time vocational programmes (including teacher training colleges,
secretarial colleges, non-graduate social work courses) while the
reverse was true of part-time job-related courses (often associated
with formal apprenticeship).

How far does this differential participation indicate a waste of
potential in terms of assessed attainment at nine years old? The
picture outlined in *Table 16* is interesting. If we look first at those
entering *full-time* courses we can see that the very small number of
children rated below average at nine who nevertheless obtained
selective school places, *all* continued in full-time education after
school. We can also see that the same is true of nearly half the
group of above average girls who did *not* obtain a grammar or

Table 16 *Recruitment to further education/training courses by sex, type of secondary school and attainment at nine years*

secondary school attended	teachers' assessment of attainment at nine years		
	above average	average	below average
full-time courses			
non-selective:			
boys	1 (11.1)	11 (17.7)	8 (9.4)
girls	7 (46.7)	19 (19.2)	5 (9.6)
grammar:			
boys	20 (55.6)	13 (54.2)	2 (100.0)
girls	22 (68.8)	10 (52.6)	2 (100.0)
technical:			
boys	1 (33.3)	7 (46.7)	1 (100.0)
girls	– (–)	5 (83.3)	no cases
part-time courses			
non-selective:			
boys	7 (77.8)	26 (41.9)	31 (36.5)
girls	2 (13.3)	31 (31.3)	16 (30.8)
grammar:			
boys	13 (36.1)	7 (29.2)	– (–)
girls	3 (9.4)	3 (15.8)	– (–)
technical:			
boys	1 (33.3)	6 (40.0)	– (–)
girls	– (–)	– (–)	no cases
apprenticeship without college attendance			
non-selective:			
boys	– (–)	9 (14.5)	18 (21.2)
girls	1 (6.7)	7 (7.1)	5 (9.6)
grammar:			
boys	2 (5.6)	1 (4.2)	– (–)
girls	3 (9.4)	2 (10.5)	– (–)
technical:			
boys	1 (33.3)	– (–)	– (–)
girls	– (–)	– (–)	no cases
no courses or training			
non-selective:			
boys	1 (11.1)	16 (25.8)	28 (32.9)
girls	5 (33.3)	42 (42.4)	26 (50.0)
grammar:			
boys	1 (2.8)	3 (12.5)	– (–)
girls	4 (12.5)	4 (21.1)	– (–)
technical:			
boys	– (–)	2 (13.0)	– (–)
girls	1 (100.0)	1 (16.7)	no cases

technical school place. The majority of the smaller group of above average boys attending non-selective school, on the other hand, went for part-time job-related courses. Also noteworthy is the increased likelihood of full-time continued education for average pupils who managed to get to grammar or technical school.

Looking at wastage of potential, very few of the above average males appear to have received no further education or training at all (two out of forty-eight, that is 4.2 per cent). Among the girls, however, the proportion rose to 20.8 per cent indicating that the loss of 'potential' noticed in recruitment to selective secondary schools was persisting. A similar, though less pronounced, sex difference emerged among pupils of average attainment at primary school.

So far we have been dealing with *recruitment* to additional education after school. It is also interesting, however, to note that 9 per cent of girls and 18 per cent of boys who started on courses failed to complete them. We might expect the highest fall-out rate to be among those who had attended non-selective schools and, in fact, this was true for the girls (19 per cent compared with 7 per cent of those entering courses from grammar school and none of the five relevant technical school girls). Among the boys, however, nearly a third (32 per cent) of the technical school boys undertaking post-school courses failed to complete them as did one in four (25 per cent) of non-selective school pupils and nearly one in five (19 per cent) of those from grammar schools. For each type of school, then, though girls might be less likely to take up further training opportunities, those girls who did were more likely to persist for the full course.

QUALIFICATIONS GAINED AFTER SCHOOL

Of those who completed the first courses they entered, 50 per cent of the boys gained 'skilled trade' qualifications and 30 per cent degrees (19 per cent) or non-degree professional qualification (11 per cent). A few boys went to college to gain O-levels (4 per cent) or A-levels (3 per cent) and about 10 per cent completed courses which did not lead to any qualification. Among the girls nearly a third of those completing courses (31 per cent) obtained 'office' qualifications (that is typing, shorthand, book-keeping, and so on.) As might be expected from the types of courses entered, less than half as many girls (8 per cent) as boys (19 per cent) obtained degrees and twice as many (22 per cent: 11 per cent) obtained non-degree professional qualifications. Relatively few girls (8 per cent) finished up with a skilled trade (mainly hairdressing), a few got O-levels (5 per cent) or A-levels (4 per cent), and a surprisingly large proportion (21 per cent) completed courses leading to no qualification whatsoever.

Among the boys, *all* those obtaining degrees came from grammar or technical school as did all but one of the female graduates. Slightly more non-selective school pupils obtained non-degree professional qualifications but, in the main, these were still restricted to the grammar and technical school populations (four out of five males; two out of three females professionally qualified). Conversely more than 80 per cent of those qualifying as skilled tradesmen (boys) or office workers (girls) came from the non-selective schools (but note that these figures are only slightly up on those expected in view of the large proportion of the group – 65 per cent boys: 73 per cent girls – attending such schools).

So far we have considered only the first course taken after leaving school and for 53 per cent of the males and 62 per cent of females concerned, this was the *only* course. A third of the boys (33 per cent) and more than a quarter (27 per cent) of the girls starting one course, however, went on to a second and 14 and 11 per cent respectively undertook three or more courses. Some of these people attempting second and third courses failed to qualify on their first attempt. Before going on to look at their working careers it is therefore of some interest to see what were the *highest* qualifications gained by members of the group by the time they were twenty-six years old, as shown in *Table 17*. It should be remembered, however, that in view of the relative youth of the group, this should not be taken as representing the final outcome.

Table 17   *Highest qualifications obtained by date of follow-up*

type of qualification	males (N=246)	females (N=238)
postgraduate research degree	3 (1.2)	1 (0.4)
postgraduate vocational qualification	12 (4.9)	5 (2.1)
degree	14 (5.7)	7 (2.9)
professional non-graduate qualification	34 (13.8)	31 (13.0)
technical/skilled trade qualification (i.e. ONC or higher)	65 (26.4)	14 (5.9)
secretarial (typing, etc) certificates	3 (1.2)	40 (16.8)
completed apprenticeship (no national certificates)	18 (7.3)	21 (8.8)
miscellaneous	10 (4.1)	9 (3.4)
no qualifications yet	87 (35.4)	111 (46.6)

Some people were still in the process of getting further qualifications. Relating these data to type of school we find, for the boys, those from non-selective schools have finished up with 'skilled' or technical qualifications (42 per cent with ONC or higher, 14 per cent completed apprenticeships 'on the job'), a small proportion (9 per cent) had professional/degree qualifications, and nearly a third (32 per cent) had no qualifications whatsoever. The more highly qualified boys predominantly came from grammar or technical school. A similar picture emerged among the girls reflecting the type of courses attended.

— 3

EMPLOYMENT

By 1977 all but three of our respondents had completed their full-time education and entered employment. For most this occurred in the late 1960s – for those attending longer college or university courses, the early 1970s. Consequently they emerged into a world where unemployment had not yet become a problem so that only 8 per cent of the females and 5 per cent of the males had failed to find their first 'permanent' job (as distinct from temporary vacation work) within three months of completing their education. The majority, particularly of those who went straight from school to work rather than further education, found a job immediately while most of those who delayed their entry to employment appeared to do so from choice: because they were waiting for a particular job, because they wanted to travel first, or, in the case of some girls, because of domestic commitments. Only five women and three men said they had been 'unemployed' before finding a job.

Table 18 *Socio-economic status of first job by secondary school type and sex*

type of secondary school	socio-economic status of first job					
	not known or no job yet	professional administrative executive managerial	intermediate (supervisory technical etc.)	routine non-manual minor supervisory	skilled manual trade	other manual
boys						
grammar	2 (3.1)	25 (39.1)	16 (25.0)	11 (17.2)	8 (12.5)	2 (3.1)
technical	1 (4.8)	6 (28.6)	3 (14.3)	6 (28.6)	5 (23.8)	– (–)
secondary modern	– (–)	4 (2.5)	6 (3.7)	18 (11.2)	98 (60.9)	35 (21.7)
total	3 (1.2)	35 (14.2)	25 (10.2)	35 (14.2)	111 (45.1)	37 (15.0)
girls						
grammar	2 (3.6)	8 (14.3)	21 (37.5)	23 (41.1)	– (–)	2 (3.6)
technical	– (–)	1 (14.3)	5 (71.4)	1 (14.3)	– (–)	– (–)
secondary modern	3 (1.7)	3 (1.7)	27 (15.4)	116 (66.3)	7 (4.0)	19 (10.9)
total	5 (2.1)	12 (5.0)	53 (22.3)	140 (58.8)	7 (2.9)	21 (8.8)

FINDING A JOB

The *type of job* entered, as might be expected, related strongly to the type of education received (see *Table 18*). The *main reasons for choosing* the first job, however, were remarkably constant regardless of sex, age of leaving school, or type of school attended, and comprised (in rough order of popularity) (i) 'it was the kind of work I wanted to do' (68 per cent females; 60 per cent males); (ii) 'it had good prospects' (53 per cent females; 61 per cent males); (iii) 'I had heard it was a good firm to work for' (43 per cent females; 33 per cent males); (iv) 'it was the first job I was offered' (36 per cent females; 39 per cent males) and (v) 'the starting pay was good' (30 per cent females; 22 per cent males). Asked to choose the single most important reason, however, all but the first of these fell away so that while 53 per cent of females and 43 per cent of males said that their *main* reason was 'it was the kind of work I wanted to do', only 11 per cent of women and 12 per cent of men mentioned the second most popular 'main choice' of 'good prospects', and 7 per cent of each sex said 'it was the first job I was offered'. Fewer than 5 per cent mentioned any other single factor, such as 'good pay'.

These young people, then, present a picture (albeit a retrospective one) of choosing their first job with some care, having clear ideas about the kind of work they wanted to do, and considering the long-term prospects as well as the immediate working conditions provided by their first job

SOCIO-ECONOMIC STATUS OF JOBS

As might be expected (and is clearly shown in *Table 18*) the types of work entered by our respondents varied widely, varying from unskilled labouring to the more prestigious of the professions. It is equally clear from looking at the 'totals' rows that there were considerable sex differences in job selection. Thus while 60 per cent of the men started out in manual jobs – predominantly skilled

.trades – only 12 per cent of the women did so. The proportions entering routine white-collar jobs were almost completely reversed. It is also noticeable that the men were three times as likely as women to start out in the most prestigious job category; the more highly qualified women began lower – in the 'intermediate' (slightly less responsible) jobs where they predominated.

Sex, then, was certainly an important factor in determining occupation and, as *Table 18* shows, sex differences occurred even when type of school attended was held constant. Thus, even if she attended a grammar school, a girl was more than twice as likely as her male counterpart to start in a routine non-manual job and less than half as likely to enter the ranks of the higher professionals, administrators, managers, and so on. For men, the type of school attended related strongly to the type of job entered so that while nearly two out of every three ex-grammar school boys started out at least in the *intermediate* ranks of white-collar workers, fewer than half of those attending technical schools did so and only one in twelve of those at non-selective schools. Conversely four out of every five boys at secondary modern schools became manual workers (and about a quarter of these went into semi-skilled or un-skilled jobs) compared with a quarter of those attending technical schools (all to skilled trades) and even fewer ex-grammar school pupils.

Among the women the picture is much less clearcut. The tendency for girls, as a whole, to enter routine non-manual jobs is reflected both among those from grammar schools and those from non-selective schools. Most 'successful' in terms of moving out of this rut were those girls who had attended technical schools (who had received their basic job training at school and therefore perhaps started at an advantage) but the numbers in this category are very small and any attempt to generalize from them might be misleading. It is also evident that both grammar and technical school ex-pupils were more likely than those from secondary moderns to start at 'intermediate' level or higher though the difference between grammar school and secondary modern is less marked than was the case with the males.

In pointing to the relationship between type of school and the type of job first entered, we are, however, perhaps over-simplifying the situation. It is often suggested that our society is not yet totally 'open' and that job opportunities may relate to social background as well as educational experiences and qualifications. And indeed we have already seen in Chapter 2 that social background, in terms of fathers' occupations, had some influence on selection for a particular type of school. *Table 19*, therefore, shows the effects of fathers' occupations (when respondents were nine years of age) on job recruitment among those educated at a similar type of school.

The fathers' jobs are shown in terms of five status groups, as before. To simplify analysis we have, however, combined the two top status groups in the case of those entering their first jobs – a step seen as justified because it was felt that *entry* to work in an 'intermediate' capacity in one's first job might well be a step towards recruitment to a higher status later (that is a temporary status).

Looking first at the totals for each level of paternal occupation we can see that, for males, recruitment to the higher non-manual jobs relates quite markedly to the father's status group. Half the sons of professional or managerial fathers started out in non-routine white-collar jobs, but only one in eight of those whose fathers were semi-skilled or unskilled manual workers and, between, we have a steady downward trend. Among the females, a similar, if slightly less marked, picture emerges.

When, however, we relate fathers' occupational status to the type of school attended, we can see that a different pattern emerges. Those who went to grammar school were likely to start work in relatively high prestige jobs regardless of their fathers' occupational status. Indeed, among the women, those whose fathers were in skilled trades or routine white-collar jobs had a higher success rate than those whose fathers were in more prestigious positions. Boys from a routine non-manual background who attended grammar school also showed a very high success rate.

The position of the small number of children from 'upper' non-manual homes who attended non-selective (secondary modern)

Table 19 Status of males' first job by father's occupational status in 1961 and type of school attended

father's status	secondary school type	respondent's status in first job				
		not known or no job	higher/ intermediate non-manual	routine non-manual	skilled manual	other manual
professional, administrative, executive, managerial	grammar	1 (5.0)	12 (60.0)	5 (25.0)	1 (5.0)	1 (5.0)
	technical	1 (33.3)	2 (66.7)	– (–)	– (–)	– (–)
	secondary modern	– (–)	1 (14.3)	2 (28.6)	1 (14.3)	3 (42.9)
	total	2 (6.7)	15 (50.0)	7 (23.3)	2 (6.7)	4 (13.3)
intermediate non-manual (supervisory, technical, etc.)	grammar	– (–)	5 (62.5)	2 (25.0)	– (–)	1 (12.5)
	technical	– (–)	2 (66.7)	1 (33.3)	– (–)	– (–)
	secondary modern	– (–)	1 (9.1)	– (–)	6 (54.5)	4 (36.4)
	total	– (–)	8 (36.4)	3 (13.6)	6 (27.3)	5 (22.7)
routine non-manual and minor supervisory	grammar	1 (12.5)	6 (75.0)	1 (12.5)	– (–)	– (–)
	technical	– (–)	1 (50.0)	1 (50.0)	– (–)	– (–)
	secondary modern	– (–)	1 (3.6)	2 (7.1)	22 (78.6)	3 (10.7)
	total	1 (2.6)	8 (21.1)	4 (10.5)	22 (57.9)	3 (7.9)
skilled manual	grammar	– (–)	10 (62.5)	2 (12.5)	4 (25.0)	– (–)
	technical	– (–)	1 (14.3)	4 (57.1)	2 (28.6)	– (–)
	secondary modern	– (–)	6 (11.3)	6 (11.3)	29 (54.7)	12 (22.6)
	total	– (–)	17 (22.4)	12 (15.8)	35 (46.1)	12 (15.8)
other manual	grammar	– (–)	6 (60.0)	1 (10.0)	3 (30.0)	– (–)
	technical	– (–)	1 (25.0)	– (–)	3 (75.0)	– (–)
	secondary modern	– (–)	1 (2.0)	6 (12.0)	35 (70.0)	8 (16.0)
	total	– (–)	8 (12.5)	7 (10.9)	41 (64.1)	8 (12.5)
not known	grammar	– (–)	2 (100.0)	– (–)	– (–)	– (–)
	technical	– (–)	2 (100.0)	– (–)	– (–)	– (–)
	secondary modern	– (–)	– (–)	2 (16.7)	5 (41.7)	5 (41.7)
	total	– (–)	4 (25.0)	2 (12.5)	5 (31.3)	5 (31.3)

Table 19—continued *Status of females' first job by father's occupational status in 1961 and type of school attended*

father's status	secondary school type	respondent's status in first job				
		not known or no job	higher/ intermediate non-manual	routine non-manual	skilled manual	other manual
professional, administrative, executive, managerial	grammar	1 (6.7)	7 (46.7)	6 (40.0)	–(–)	1 (6.7)
	technical	–(–)	1 (100.0)	–(–)	–(–)	–(–)
	secondary modern	1 (10.0)	4 (40.0)	5 (50.0)	–(–)	–(–)
	total	2 (7.7)	12 (46.2)	11 (42.3)	–(–)	1 (3.8)
intermediate non-manual (supervisory, technical, etc.)	grammar	–(–)	6 (46.2)	5 (38.5)	–(–)	1 (7.7)
	technical	–(–)	2 (100.0)	–(–)	–(–)	–(–)
	secondary modern	–(–)	5 (25.0)	14 (70.0)	–(–)	1 (5.0)
	total	1 (2.9)	13 (37.1)	19 (54.3)	–(–)	2 (5.7)
routine non-manual and minor supervisory	grammar	–(–)	6 (60.0)	4 (40.0)	–(–)	–(–)
	technical	–(–)	1 (100.0)	–(–)	–(–)	–(–)
	secondary modern	–(–)	4 (15.4)	19 (73.1)	2 (7.7)	1 (3.8)
	total	–(–)	11 (29.7)	23 (62.2)	2 (5.4)	1 (2.7)
skilled manual	grammar	–(–)	6 (75.0)	2 (25.0)	–(–)	–(–)
	technical	–(–)	1 (50.0)	1 (50.0)	–(–)	–(–)
	secondary modern	1 (1.9)	12 (23.1)	30 (57.7)	2 (3.8)	7 (13.5)
	total	1 (1.6)	19 (30.6)	33 (53.2)	2 (3.2)	7 (11.3)
other manual	grammar	–(–)	3 (42.9)	4 (57.1)	–(–)	–(–)
	technical	–(–)	1 (100.0)	–(–)	–(–)	–(–)
	secondary modern	1 (2.1)	4 (8.5)	32 (68.1)	3 (6.4)	7 (14.9)
	total	1 (1.8)	8 (14.5)	36 (65.5)	3 (5.5)	7 (12.7)
non known	grammar	–(–)	1 (33.3)	2 (66.7)	–(–)	–(–)
	technical	–(–)	–(–)	–(–)	–(–)	–(–)
	secondary modern	–(–)	1 (5.0)	16 (80.0)	–(–)	3 (15.0)
	total	–(–)	2 (8.7)	18 (78.3)	–(–)	3 (13.0)

schools is also interesting. It is from this group of males that we have the highest recruitment to routine non-manual jobs and to semi-skilled or unskilled manual ones, while the proportion going into skilled trades is very low.

Also interesting is the high level of recruitment to skilled manual work which occurs among the sons of routine non-manual workers, that is eight out of ten of those attending secondary modern schools compared with only just over half of similarly educated boys whose fathers were themselves in skilled trades.

Among the women, the tendency for jobs to peak in the less prestigious white-collar area makes analysis more difficult. Even allowing for this, however, the situation is much less clearcut than that among the men. Among the daughters of the most prestigiously occupied men, for example, those who attended secondary modern schools appeared to do as well occupationally as those with grammar school education, though this was not the case elsewhere. Entry to manual jobs was rare for girls whose fathers were in professional, managerial, or intermediate white-collar jobs (where two out of the three girls concerned had attended grammar school) but thereafter increased gradually among secondary modern school leavers to a peak of 21 per cent among those with semi-skilled or unskilled fathers.

Returning to personal/educational qualifications of the respondents themselves, *Table 20* shows that performance in the examination stakes at school provides a good predictor of the point of entry to the job market so that four out of five of the males with three or more A-level passes, and only marginally fewer females, started work in the intermediate or higher range of white-collar jobs. Among the men, the greater part of the most highly qualified in fact started their working life in professional or managerial positions. Among the women, as we might expect from previous analysis, not only did a smaller percentage get three or more A-levels but also, of those who did, fewer started at the top. A similar sex difference existed for all levels of qualifications with the women twice as likely as the men to start out in the intermediate white-collar category.

Table 20 *Number of A-Level passes obtained at school by status of first job and sex*

number of A-Level passes	status of first job					
	profes-sional adminis-trative managerial	inter-mediate white collar	routine white collar	skilled manual	other manual	not known or no job yet
boys						
none	7 (3.5)	18 (9.0)	28 (14.1)	110 (55.3)	35 (17.6)	1 (0.5)
1 or 2	7 (41.2)	4 (25.3)	3 (17.6)	– (–)	2 (11.8)	1 (5.9)
3 or more	21 (70.0)	3 (10.0)	4 (13.3)	1 (3.3)	– (–)	1 (3.3)
girls						
none	2 (1.0)	37 (18.3)	135 (66.8)	7 (3.5)	19 (9.4)	2 (1.0)
1 or 2	4 (19.0)	11 (52.4)	2 (9.5)	– (–)	2 (9.5)	2 (9.5)
3 or more	6 (40.0)	5 (33.3)	3 (20.0)	– (–)	– (–)	1 (6.7)

At the opposite end of the scale, *Table 20* shows that those with no A-levels tended to be recruited to manual jobs, mainly skilled trades if male, routine white-collar jobs if female. There was also, however, some recruitment of apparently unqualified people to high status jobs. At first sight this may seem surprising but the explanation lies in the specificity of the table. The possession of A-level passes is *normally* a prerequisite for entry to further education and training and such passes are *usually* gained at school. It is possible, however, for people to gain qualifications at further education colleges between leaving school and starting work – a path followed by those whose schools cannot take them further than the basic O-level examinations and those who prefer the more relaxed atmosphere of the colleges. This accounts for most of the apparently unqualified males and one of the women entering professional or managerial jobs. The rest (that is two males and one female) had obtained other types of qualifications while at school.

Table 21 looks at the relationship between the top qualifications gained by the age of twenty-six and the status of the person's first job. Again it must be stressed that, though most people gained these qualifications *before* starting work, there were some few

Table 21   *Top qualifications gained after school by sex and status of first job*

qualifications gained	social status of first job					
	profes-sional managerial	inter-mediate white collar	routine white collar	skilled manual	other manual	not known or no job yet
boys						
degree	22 (75.9)	2 (6.9)	4 (13.8)	– (–)	– (–)	1 (3.4)
other professional technical[1]	9 (26.5)	12 (35.3)	5 (14.7)	8 (23.5)	– (–)	– (–)
or clerical	2 (2.3)	3 (3.5)	6 (7.0)	67 (77.9)	8 (9.3)	– (–)
none	2 (2.1)	8 (8.2)	19 (19.6)	34 (35.1)	29 (29.9)	5 (5.2)
girls						
degree	8 (61.5)	1 (7.7)	4 (30.8)	– (–)	– (–)	– (–)
other professional technical	3 (9.7)	14 (45.2)	10 (32.3)	– (–)	2 (6.4)	2 (6.4)
or clerical	– (–)	24 (32.0)	45 (60.0)	4 (5.3)	2 (2.7)	– (–)
none	1 (0.8)	14 (11.8)	81 (68.1)	3 (2.5)	17 (14.3)	3 (2.5)

Note: [1] Including completion of an apprenticeship with training on the job.

exceptions; for example those who gained accountancy qualifications by part-time study while working in offices.

Here again the sex differences are striking. Not only, as we have already seen, were women less likely to have degrees (and more likely to take other professional training, for example nursing, education, medical auxiliary) but also, even if they did get a degree, they were still more likely to start work in a routine white-collar capacity than were men. Nevertheless, in each sex, the possession of a degree or other professional qualification did, on the whole, act as a passport to the more prestigious (intermediate and above) levels of white-collar work. Without such qualifications entry was relatively rare among the men although possession of secretarial qualifications did appear to ensure an increased recruitment to the 'intermediate' white-collar levels for women.

The close relationship between qualifications and job type is scarcely surprising since one of the factors underlying the status gradation of jobs was the amount and type of training required, the 'top' jobs being those requiring the longest full-time specialized training; university-type education is also usually involved while those trained elsewhere (colleges of education, technical colleges) are rated 'lower'. Consequently, in comparing job status with type of education/qualifications it may be said that our argument is circular; jobs requiring one type of training/qualification are seen as 'superior' to those requiring another type and so those jobs can *demand* certain entry criteria. Their prestige is then reinforced by the fact that they *do* place such restrictions on entry. In the same way, it can be argued that the lack of women in the highest status jobs owes something to the lower status given to jobs (often requiring equal length of training) where women predominate.

Leaving 'status' out of account, however, it is obvious that women in the late 1960s and early 1970s were still being recruited to different types of jobs from men even when their qualifications were similar. The working world entered by women is not the same as that entered by men of equivalent education or qualifications. As we will see, these differences do not become any less as we trace our respondents through the first ten (or fewer) years of their working lives.

STABILITY OF EMPLOYMENT

Once they had entered employment most people stayed in it for some time. Only 13 per cent of women and 10 per cent of men changed their jobs within the first six months while two-fifths of the women (39 per cent) and half the men (49 per cent) had remained with their first employer for at least three years. By the date of the follow-up survey, however, when they were twenty-six years old, most of our respondents (89 per cent of women and 82 per cent of men) had moved on. As *Table 22* ('total' column) shows, the main reason given by both men and women for leaving their first job was either that they had disliked some aspect of that job (prospects, pay, conditions, hours) or that they had found something better. Relatively few young people left their first job involuntarily because the job folded up (10 per cent of men; 8 per

Table 22 *Reasons for leaving first job by main reason for taking it by sex*

reasons for leaving first job	main reasons for taking first job					total
	it was the job desired	first or only job offered	good prospects	good firm, good pay	other	
girls						
not applicable: still there	16 (12.6)	5 (18.5)	2 (8.0)	3 (16.7)	1 (2.5)	27 (11.4)
disliked the job	29 (22.8)	6 (22.2)	5 (20.0)	5 (27.8)	10 (25.0)	55 (23.2)
moved to a better job	26 (20.5)	7 (25.9)	6 (24.0)	3 (16.7)	13 (32.5)	55 (23.2)
domestic reasons	23 (18.1)	5 (18.5)	5 (20.0)	4 (22.2)	5 (12.5)	42 (17.7)
left the area	12 (9.4)	1 (3.7)	3 (12.0)	– (–)	4 (10.0)	20 (8.4)
job disappeared (redundancy, etc.)	8 (6.3)	2 (7.4)	2 (8.0)	2 (11.1)	4 (10.0)	18 (7.6)
sacked, left after argument	4 (3.1)	1 (3.7)	1 (4.0)	– (–)	– (–)	6 (2.5)
other reasons	7 (5.5)	– (–)	– (–)	– (–)	2 (5.0)	9 (3.8)
reasons n.k.	2 (1.6)	– (–)	1 (4.0)	1 (5.6)	1 (2.5)	5 (2.1)
total	127 (99.9)	27 (99.9)	25 (100.0)	18 (100.1)	40 (100.0)	237 (99.9)
boys						
not applicable: still there	21 (20.0)	3 (8.6)	7 (23.3)	5 (29.4)	9 (15.8)	45 (18.4)
disliked the job	30 (28.6)	11 (31.4)	9 (30.0)	5 (29.4)	13 (22.8)	68 (27.9)
moved to a better job	30 (28.6)	14 (40.0)	7 (23.3)	1 (5.9)	16 (28.1)	68 (27.9)
domestic reasons	1 (1.0)	– (–)	– (–)	– (–)	– (–)	1 (0.4)
left the area	– (–)	1 (2.9)	– (–)	– (–)	2 (3.5)	3 (1.2)
job disappeared (redundancy, etc.)	13 (12.4)	2 (5.7)	3 (10.0)	1 (5.9)	5 (8.8)	24 (9.8)
sacked, left after argument	6 (5.7)	3 (8.6)	1 (3.3)	1 (5.9)	5 (8.8)	16 (6.6)
other reasons	2 (1.9)	– (–)	3 (10.0)	3 (17.6)	6 (10.5)	14 (5.7)
reasons n.k.	2 (1.9)	1 (2.9)	– (–)	1 (5.9)	1 (1.8)	5 (2.0)
total	105 (100.1)	35 (100.1)	30 (99.9)	17 (100.0)	57 (100.1)	244 (99.9)

cent of women) and even fewer because they were sacked or left as the result of an argument with the 'boss' (7 per cent of men; 3 per cent of women).

The main sex differences, however, lie in the proportion of people who said they left their first job for 'domestic' reasons (forty-two women and one man) or because they were leaving the area (as a result of a family move or setting up home in a new area on marriage, for instance). Thus one in four of the women left their first job because of factors unconnected (explicitly at least) with that job or with their 'career' in paid employment. If these women are omitted from our analysis the sex differences relating to other reasons for leaving the first job tend to disappear.

To what extent did reasons for leaving their first job relate to the reasons given for taking it originally? Would it have been possible to make predictions? So far as the women were concerned, the answer appears to have been 'no'. Indeed, the only column in *Table 22* showing any variation comprises the miscellaneous group who gave 'other' (very mixed) reasons for choosing their first job and who show a greater 'career' orientation. Among the men, however, those who took the first or only job offered seemed less likely to stay in it and more likely to move to what they saw as a 'better' job. Conversely those who chose their first job on grounds of good conditions or good pay were markedly the least likely to see their move as taking them to 'better' things and (marginally) the most likely to have stayed with the same firm.

SUBSEQUENT WORK HISTORY

By the time they were twenty-six, most of our respondents (87 per cent of men and 75 per cent of women) had been in paid employment for at least five years. As *Table 23* shows, the sex difference apparent here becomes more obvious when we look at those working the maximum possible years (nine or more). Of the men who left school at fifteen or sixteen, 86 per cent had worked ever since, but this was true of only 40 per cent of similar women. The

Table 23   *Number of jobs held by total time spent in paid employment by sex*

total duration of paid employment	no. of jobs held					
	nil	1	2–4	5–10	11 or more	total
men						
less than 3 yrs	–	2	1	–	–	3
	(–)	(66.7)	(33.3)	(–)	(–)	(100.0)
3–4 yrs	–	8	11	2	–	21
	(–)	(38.1)	(52.4)	(9.5)	(–)	(100.1)
5–8 yrs	–	9	25	16	–	50
	(–)	(18.0)	(50.0)	(32.0)	(–)	(100.0)
9 or more yrs	–	26	73	57	8	164
	(–)	(15.9)	(44.5)	(34.8)	(4.9)	(100.0)
duration not known	–	–	1	2	3	6
	(–)	(–)	(17.7)	(33.3)	(50.0)	(100.0)
no job yet	2	–	–	–	–	2
	(100.0)	(–)	(–)	(–)	(–)	(100.0)
total	2	45	111	77	11	246
	(0.8)	(18.3)	(45.1)	(31.3)	(4.5)	(100.0)
women						
less than 3 yrs	–	4	8	2	–	14
	(–)	(28.6)	(57.1)	(14.3)	(–)	(100.0)
3–4 yrs	–	6	25	8	1	40
	(–)	(15.0)	(62.5)	(20.0)	(2.5)	(100.0)
5–8 yrs	–	11	46	33	1	91
	(–)	(12.1)	(50.5)	(36.3)	(1.1)	(100.0)
9 or more yrs	–	17	35	36	–	88
	(–)	(19.3)	(39.8)	(40.9)	(–)	(100.0)
duration not known	–	1	2	1	–	4
	(–)	(25.0)	(50.0)	(25.0)	(–)	(100.0)
no job yet						
	(100.0)	(–)	(–)	(–)	(–)	(100.0)
total	1	39	116	80	2	238
	(0.4)	(16.4)	(48.7)	(33.6)	(0.8)	(99.9)

reason is obvious. In times of full employment such as existed during the relevant period, men, once they start work, tend to continue working apart from temporary breaks attributable to sickness, unemployment, and so on. Women, on the other hand, leave the job market for longer periods (or even permanently) because of their other roles such as home-makers and child carers.

This is of some importance when we compare the job mobility (number of jobs held) of members of each sex. As *Table 23* shows, the overall (total) figures for each sex are not dissimilar, with roughly a half of each group having held two or four jobs and a third, five or more. When we look at numbers of jobs held in relation to total time at work, however, we can see that this overall similarity can be misleading. Thus, if we look at those with the shortest working lives, we can see that 42 per cent of the men who had worked for less than five years had held only a single job but, among equivalent women, the figure dropped to 19 per cent while 20 per cent had changed jobs at least four times (compared with only 8 per cent of their male counterparts). Among those working nine or more years (that is those who have worked more or less continuously since leaving school) these differences largely disappear.

Women who leave the job market (temporarily or permanently) appear to have a more mobile work history than do women whose work has been continuous or men. There may be two explanations for this. One is that the demands of domestic roles *cause* job changes; the other is that dissatisfaction with working conditions may lead both to frequent job changes and to transfer out of the job market in favour of housework and child-rearing. From our investigation it is not possible to be dogmatic about which hypothesis is correct. The *reasons* given by people for leaving their jobs do, however, provide some interesting information in that 61 per cent of our female respondents had left at least one job because of marriage/pregnancy while about one in six (16 per cent) had done so more than once for these reasons. In addition, more than a quarter of the women (27 per cent) said they had changed jobs at least once *because* their home had moved. Some of these cases might, of course, relate to moves by the parental home, but it is doubtful if this accounts for the whole as only 7 per cent of men gave this reason.

Leaving a job because of marriage/pregnancy did not appear to bear any consistent relationship to educational background.

Taking school leaving age as a rough indicator, the highest proportion affected was found to occur among those leaving school at
seventeen (73 per cent) and the lowest (31 per cent) among those
staying a year longer. Similarly, while 71 per cent of those leaving
at fifteen were affected, only 59 per cent of sixteen-year-old
leavers were! This is interesting as length of time spent as a full-
time homemaker *did* relate to school leaving age (see *Table 24*) so
that while three-quarters of those leaving school at fifteen had
spent some time out of the job market by the age of twenty-six,
this was true of only a third of girls leaving school at seventeen or
older. At the other end of the scale, we can see that about one in
four of the earliest school-leavers had spent five or more years as a
full-time home-maker compared with only one in ten of those
leaving a year later and *none* of those staying until they were
seventeen. For girls who left secondary modern schools as soon as
legally possible, then, working life has undoubtedly been affected
(and curtailed) by early marriage and/or pregnancy.

So far as factors relating to work itself were concerned, however, the main reason for changing jobs in each sex, was to go to a
better one, in search of better pay, better prospects, or better
working conditions. This was particularly marked among the
men where more than half our respondents (56 per cent of men;
44 per cent of women) said they had moved for this reason at least
once and nearly a third (30 per cent of men; 16 per cent of women)
more than once. The men were also more likely to move from a
job into self-employment (11.8 per cent of men; 2.1 per cent of

Table 24   *Time spent as a full-time homemaker by age at which left school*

age left school	time spent as full-time homemaker				
	not known	*none*	*less than 2 years*	*3–4 years*	*5 or more years*
15 years	8 (6.8)	29 (24.8)	28 (24.8)	25 (21.4)	27 (23.1)
16 years	4 (5.7)	29 (41.4)	16 (22.9)	14 (20.0)	7 (10.0)
17 or later	1 (2.0)	35 (68.6)	9 (17.6)	6 (11.8)	– (–)
total	13 (5.5)	93 (39.1)	53 (22.3)	45 (18.9)	34 (14.3)

women) but *not* because of promotion within a firm (13 per cent in each sex).

Dislike of the job or working conditions was given as a reason for leaving one or more jobs by about a quarter of the men and about one in five of the women, and 'boredom' by 15 per cent in each group. The men were about twice as likely as the women to say they had been 'sacked' or left 'after an argument with the boss' (but this involved relatively few people, anyway). Redundancy or closure of the firm was mentioned by about one in five of the men but slightly fewer women (perhaps reflecting the greater likelihood of men setting up their own firms).

We have seen that the number of jobs held relates clearly to the amount of time spent in the job market, that is it reflects the age at which the person *enters* the employment sector and the age at which they leave it. We have already examined in Chapter 3 the factors which relate to prolonged education and delay in entering work. In Chapter 5 we look at factors associated with early marriage/pregnancy. We can, however, ask at this stage, whether there is any evidence that a changeable job pattern is related to any personal characteristics in terms of the reported behaviour of our respondents when they were nine years old. Was any prediction of a 'poor' work history possible? Broadly speaking, the answer is no! Among the men, no consistent association existed between 'deviation score' at nine years of age and number of jobs held apart from the increased proportion of multiple (five or more) job holders among the ten who had high deviation scores (60 per cent) and the twelve whose parents failed to complete the behaviour questionnaire in 1961 (50 per cent). These two groups were also twice as likely to have left their first job within twelve months (40 per cent and 42 per cent respectively compared with 15 per cent of deviation-free and 19 per cent of other deviation score groups). Those *least* likely to have had more than four jobs were the originally 'deviation-free' (31 per cent) and those credited with two or three deviant traits (29 per cent).

Among the women, those with the most deviant traits at nine were among the *least* likely to have had five or more jobs (30 per cent compared with 32 per cent of the deviance-free and 28 per cent of those with a score of one). Those for whom no behavioural information was available were the most likely to change jobs frequently (62 per cent). Again, however, it is necessary to consider that some women, rather than changing jobs, have dropped out of the job market, temporarily or permanently. This will be discussed further in the next chapter in relation to age at marriage, and so on. For the moment, however, we can mention that the most 'deviant' girls (that is those with scores of four or more) and those for whom no original parental information was available were the least likely to have stayed for five or more years in their first job (6 per cent of those with a deviation score of four or five; none of those with a score of six or more; and 8 per cent of those whose deviation score was not known: compared with 24 per cent of deviance-free and 28 per cent of those with low scores).

Attempting to relate number of jobs to *individual types of behaviour* reported in 1961 presents even more problems because of the small number of individuals exhibiting the 'deviant' type of behaviour in each case. One interesting relationship which *did* emerge, however, showed that 73 per cent (eight out of eleven) of those boys described as having 'very changeable moods' at nine had held five or more jobs compared with 32 per cent of those whose parents saw them as less moody.

SITUATION AT TWENTY-SIX

By the time they reached the age of twenty-six many of our respondents not only had changed their actual jobs but also had changed their occupational status. This is shown clearly in *Table 25* where, for example, more men who started life as routine white-collar workers had moved out of that type of work than remained in it.

Among the women, the most striking fact is the large-scale movement out of the labour market altogether in favour of housekeeping/child raising which had reduced the number in paid employment by 37 per cent. If we exclude these people and look only at women still employed, mobility among women is only

Table 25 *Comparison of status of first job and of job occupied at age 26*

first job type	job at age 26									
	professional, administrative (1)	managerial, executive (2)	intermediate, supervisory, technical (3)	routine white collar, minor supervisory (4, 5)	skilled manual	other manual	total working	not working (home care)	not working (other) or job unknown	total
women										
professional administrative executive,	1	–	–	–	–	–	1 (0.7)	–	–	1 (0.4)
managerial	–	10	–	–	–	–	10 (7.2)	1 (1.1)	–	11 (4.6)
intermediate	–	5	22	3	–	1	31 (22.3)	21 (23.6)	1	53 (22.7)
routine non-manual, minor manual, supervisory	1	3	16	51	–	12	83 (59.7)	54 (60.7)	3	140 (58.8)
skilled manual	–	–	–	–	–	2	2 (1.4)	3 (3.4)	2	7 (2.9)
other manual	–	2	–	5	1	4	12 (8.6)	8 (9.0)	1	21 (8.8)
not known, no job	–	–	–	–	–	–	–	2 (2.2)	3	5 (2.1)
total	2 (1.4)	20 (14.4)	38 (27.3)	59 (42.4)	1 (0.8)	19 (13.7)	189 (100.0)	89 (100.0)	10	238 (100.0)
men										
professional, administrative executive,	16	2	–	–	–	–	18 (7.7)	–	–	18 (7.3)
managerial	3	13	–	–	–	–	16 (6.9)	–	1	17 (6.9)
intermediate	–	5	16	2	1	–	24 (10.3)	–	1	25 (10.2)
routine non-manual, minor manual, supervisory	2	6	7	13	1	4	33 (14.2)	–	2	35 (14.2)
skilled manual	–	4	12	20	58	13	107 (45.9)	–	4	111 (45.1)
other manual	–	1	2	5	11	15	34 (14.6)	–	3	37 (15.0)
job not categorized	1	–	–	–	–	–	1 (0.4)	–	2	3 (1.2)
total	22 (9.4)	31 (13.3)	37 (15.9)	40 (17.2)	71 (30.5)	32 (13.7)	233 (100.0)	–	13	246 (100.0)

slightly less than that found among the men so that 88 out of the 139 women still employed (63.3 per cent) were still in the same category of jobs compared with 131 and 233 working men (56.2 per cent) whose job was known. If we include movement into domesticity, however, the women's mobility rises considerably leaving only 38.6 per cent in their original categories.

Because of upward job mobility among those working in each sex, the distribution has become flatter with the proportion of women in routine white-collar jobs and men working as skilled artisans coming down and the proportion in managerial/executive or intermediate white-collar jobs rising. This is particularly noticeable if we look in more detail at what has happened to those 111 young men who started their working life training for a skilled trade. By the time they were twenty-six just over half were still employed as skilled tradesmen and about an eighth were in semi-skilled or unskilled work. A third, however, had moved out of purely manual work either into a supervisory role (including running their own businesses) or into white-collar work. Similarly, among those men who started work in routine white-collar jobs 45 per cent had moved up into at least 'intermediate' status. Among women starting in routine white-collar work (which applied to more than half of our group) upward mobility also occurred but to a less marked extent. Of those still working at twenty-six just a quarter had moved to more supervisory posts while 60 per cent had stayed at the same status.

In each sex, the lowest mobility occurred among those who started out at high status who could not rise and who did not fall. It is also noticeable that this group (those in administrative or managerial jobs) among the women did not leave work for domesticity – only one girl (out of twelve) had done so compared with approximately 40 per cent in each of the other employment categories.

Again we must ask to what extent people's job status at the age of twenty-six could have been predicted from earlier information. Obviously we would expect type of secondary education to be important – and it was!

Table 26   *Type of job at age 26 by secondary school attended and sex*

job status at 26 yrs	men		women	
	grammar and technical school	non-selective school	grammar and technical school	non-selective school
professional, managerial	43 (49.4)	10 (6.3)	17 (27.0)	5 (2.9)
intermediate	20 (23.0)	17 (10.7)	17 (27.0)	21 (12.0)
routine white collar and minor supervisory	9 (10.3)	31 (19.5)	8 (12.7)	51 (29.1)
skilled manual	6 (6.9)	65 (40.9)	– (–)	1 (0.6)
other manual	1 (1.1)	31 (19.5)	– (–)	19 (10.9)
housewife	– (–)	– (–)	20 (31.7)	69 (39.4)
other/no job/ job unknown	8 (9.2)	5 (3.1)	1 (1.6)	9 (5.1)
total	87 (100.0)	159 (100.0)	63 (100.0)	175 (100.0)

As *Table 26* shows, among the men who had attended grammar or technical schools, half had reached at least managerial grade and only a quarter were employed at below intermediate white-collar status (most of these coming from technical schools). Conversely, only 6 per cent of ex-pupils of non-selective schools had achieved managerial status while two-fifths were still manual workers. A similar picture emerged among the women, where those who went to grammar or technical schools were nine times as likely as non-selective school pupils to have achieved managerial status and twice as likely to be in an 'intermediate' one. Not one of the women educated at grammar or technical school was in a manual job, compared with a fifth (21 per cent) of those who were still working and who attended a non-selective school.

On the whole, then, type of secondary school attended was of vital importance in determining job opportunities. Some people without the appropriate background had, however, made it into the 'top' jobs and it seemed of some interest to find out how this had happened.

There appeared to be two paths. The first, shown in *Table 27*, was to acquire qualifications *after* leaving school. This accounted for most of the people who had reached intermediate, managerial, or professional status by the age of twenty-six despite attending a secondary modern school. An example is George A. who, when he left school, started his working life as an engineering apprentice but left after two years as he found the work boring. He enrolled

Table 27 *Latest job of those attending non-selective schools by qualifications gained since leaving school*

job at 26	highest qualification gained since leaving school				
	profes-sional	technical (HNC/ONC)	office skills (eg. RSA)	O-levels A-levels and misc. courses eg. music	no formal qualifica-tions recorded
men					
professional, administrative managerial	3 (30.0)	– (–)	– (–)	4 (40.0)	3 (30.0)
intermediate	4 (23.5)	11 (64.7)	– (–)	– (–)	2 (11.8)
routine white collar and minor supervisory	– (–)	15 (48.4)	– (–)	1 (3.2)	15 (48.4)
skilled manual	– (–)	29 (44.6)	1 (1.5)	2 (3.1)	33 (50.8)
other manual	– (–)	2 (6.5)	– (–)	1 (3.2)	28 (90.3)
no job/job not known	– (–)	1 (14.3)	– (–)	– (–)	6 (85.7)
total	7 (4.3)	58 (36.0)	1 (0.6)	8 (5.0)	87 (54.0)
women					
managerial	2 (40.0)	1 (20.0)	– (–)	– (–)	2 (40.0)
intermediate	4 (19.0)	–	9 (42.9)	1 (4.8)	7 (33.3)
routine white collar and minor supervisory	2 (3.9)	4 (7.8)	10 (19.6)	1 (2.0)	34 (66.7)
manual	– (–)	– (–)	4 (20.0)	– (–)	16 (80.0)
not employed	4 (5.5)	3 (4.1)	9 (12.3)	1 (1.4)	56 (76.7)
not known	– (–)	– (–)	1 (20.0)	– (–)	4 (80.0)
total	12 (6.9)	8 (4.6)	33 (18.9)	3 (1.7)	119 (68.0)

in a college of further education and acquired three A-levels including one in economics. This helped him get a job as a sales representative. Two changes of job later he had become area sales manager for a large company. In the same way, three men who started work as routine clerks had subsequently, by part-time study, acquired accountancy qualifications.

The other way (not necessarily separate) was by promotion within a firm or organization. Thus people were promoted in banks from junior clerks to cashiers; in other offices or shops they rose from routine work to supervisor. In some cases this promotion was the result of acquiring qualifications – in others, it seemed to reflect experience and individual ability. Some people, then, succeeded by perseverance and ability even though they had been penalized by a selective educational system. There still remains, however, the question of wastage of potential.

As we saw in the chapter on education, teachers' assessments of attainment at nine years of age were closely related to selection for secondary education, but there was some overlap. In *Table 28* we have looked at the influence on job success of perceived early attainment as well as type of secondary school attended and find that the school appeared the more important factor in determining job potential. Boys seen by their teachers as 'average', or even 'below average', in attainment, if they managed to get to a technical school or, even more so, a grammar school were likely to achieve the 'top' occupationally by the time they were twenty-six. Conversely, those few boys seen as 'above average' at nine who, nevertheless, did not attend selective schools were to be found mainly in routine white-collar or minor supervisory jobs or working as skilled tradesmen.

A rather larger proportion of girls of 'above average' attainment at nine failed to get a place at grammar or technical school (see also p. 29). We therefore already have what may be seen as a substantial wastage of potential. On the other hand, we have seen that the jobs entered by women tend to be more closely grouped than those of men leading to less job differentation between those of differing educational background.

Table 28 *Type of job at age 26 by secondary school type, attainment at 9 years*

job status at age 26 yrs	grammar and technical school				non-selective schools			
	above average	average	below average	total[1]	above average	average	below average	total[1]
men								
professional, managerial	21 (53.8)	20 (48.8)	1 (33.3)	43 (49.4)	1 (11.1)	3 (5.0)	5 (5.9)	10 (6.3)
intermediate	9 (23.1)	8 (19.5)	2 (66.7)	20 (23.0)	1 (11.1)	8 (13.3)	7 (8.2)	17 (10.7)
routine white collar and minor supervisory	3 (7.8)	5 (12.2)	–(–)	9 (10.3)	4 (44.4)	12 (20.0)	15 (17.6)	31 (19.5)
skilled manual	4 (10.3)	1 (2.4)	–(–)	6 (6.9)	3 (33.3)	26 (43.3)	33 (38.8)	65 (40.9)
other manual	–(–)	1 (2.4)	–(–)	1 (1.1)	–(–)	9 (15.0)	22 (25.9)	31 (19.5)
no job/job not known	2 (5.1)	6 (14.6)	–(–)	8 (9.2)	–(–)	2 (3.3)	3 (3.5)	5 (3.1)
total	39	41	3	87	9	60	85	159
women								
professional, managerial	9 (27.3)	5 (20.0)	3 (60.0)	17 (27.0)	1 (6.7)	4 (4.0)	–(–)	5 (2.9)
intermediate	7 (21.2)	10 (40.0)	–(–)	17 (27.0)	4 (26.7)	13 (13.1)	4 (7.7)	21 (12.0)
routine white collar and minor supervisory	4 (12.1)	3 (12.0)	1 (20.0)	8 (12.7)	6 (40.0)	26 (26.3)	16 (30.8)	51 (29.1)
manual	–(–)	–(–)	–(–)	–(–)	–(–)	14 (14.1)	6 (11.5)	20 (11.4)
at home	12 (36.4)	7 (78.0)	1 (20.0)	20 (31.7)	4 (26.7)	36 (36.4)	24 (46.2)	69 (39.4)
other/not employed or job not known	1 (3.0)	–(–)	–(–)	1 (1.6)	–(–)	6 (6.1)	2 (3.8)	9 (5.1)
total	33	25	5	63	15	99	52	175

Note: [1] Totals include those whose attainment at nine years was not recorded and, therefore, may exceed the sum of the period of the previous three columns.

Looking first at 'wastage' in terms of those who have quitted employment (temporarily or permanently) for child-rearing and/or home care we can see, first, that the overall difference is small between those educated at secondary modern schools and those with grammar/technical school education. If we look *within* each educational group, however, more variation becomes apparent and, furthermore, the trends within each group operate in different directions. Thus, among women educated at secondary modern schools, those with the *lowest* attainment at nine are the most likely to have stopped work (46.2 per cent) while the most able are the least likely to have done so (26.7 per cent) and the 'average' take up a medium position (36.4 per cent). Among those who 'passed' into grammar or technical school, however, the opposite is true and the 'high' attainers at nine are the most likely to have become full-time housewives (36.4 per cent).

If we look at the women in employment we can see that, once again, those who went to grammar or technical school were much more likely to have reached the top positions, regardless of attainment at nine years of age. Among those seen as 'above average' who subsequently went to a non-selective school only one (9 per cent of those working) had a job of at least managerial status. Among women of equivalent potential educated at grammar or technical school, 45 per cent of those still employed were in such appointments. Conversely, more than half (54.5 per cent) of the girls of 'above average' attainment who went on to secondary modern school, and were still working in 1978, were employed in minor supervisory or routine office jobs in comparison with only 20 per cent of those of apparently equal potential at the age of nine who were successful in the eleven-plus procedures. As can be seen from *Table 28* differences in the other attainment groups are equally striking, showing the great effect which selective secondary education can have in determining an individual's 'life chance' in terms of occupational status.

— 4 —
FAMILY AND MARRIAGE

FAMILY OF ORIGIN

In 1961 when they were nine years old, the majority of people were apparently living in 'normal' two-parent homes (91 per cent of boys; 90 per cent of girls). Three in each sex were living with their mothers only and two boys with their fathers. One boy and two girls were being brought up by their grandparents; two girls were in long-term foster homes; one girl was with adoptive parents and one boy was living in a children's home.

However these figures may well be an underestimate of the actual family disruption experienced. For one thing, we do not know anything about the situation in the families who did not fill in their forms in 1961 and there is reason to believe that family problems (parental illness or absence, say) might have contributed to non-cooperation in at least some cases. Secondly, the information about family background collected in 1961 was far from comprehensive so that we do not know for sure whether the persons referred to as 'mother' and 'father' are the biological parents or whether they are adopted parents, step-parents, for example. In some instances this information was provided spontaneously but this may not always have been the case.

We do know that about one in four of the boys (24.3 per cent) and one in five of the girls (18.5 per cent) had experienced some period of separation owing to the absence of one parent (or, in a very few cases, both parents) for a period lasting at least a week. The absent parent was rather more likely to be the father (forty-two boys; twenty-five girls) compared with twenty-two boys and twenty-one girls whose mother had been away.

The number of children who, themselves, had had to leave home for at least a week (excluding hospitalization which is covered in Chapter 6) was much smaller with only four boys and two girls spending time in a children's home (though half were there on two or more occasions) and three boys and two girls placed with foster parents. Rather more usual, in times of family stress, was a prolonged stay with relatives (six boys, seven girls) while three girls and six boys (not counting those adopted or fostered from birth) had moved to a new permanent 'home' at some stage in their first nine years.

Few of the group were still 'only children' at nine (9.3 per cent boys; 10.1 per cent girls) while more than a quarter (24.2 per cent boys; 28.2 per cent girls) had three or more siblings. They were spread fairly regularly through the family with 30 per cent being the eldest, 25 per cent youngest, and 29 per cent in the middle. Only three boys were part of a pair of twins.

As might be expected from the spread of family size and position, parental ages also covered quite a wide range though few (one father, ten mothers) were aged less than twenty when the child was born and few (three fathers) over fifty. Most mothers had been in their twenties (61 per cent) with fathers slightly older so that 41 per cent were in their twenties, 43 per cent in their thirties.

The social spread (see also Chapter 2), though peaking at the skilled manual level, was also wide with 12 per cent having fathers in the more prestigious professional and administrative types of job while the fathers of 26 per cent were in semi-skilled or un-skilled work.

So far as mothers were concerned 39 per cent said that they had a job, mainly a part-time one (83 per cent of these working); only 24 women were working full-time in employment outside the home.

By the time they were fifteen, twelve boys and four girls were living with only one parent; six boys and one girl were living in some sort of institutional setting (children's home, approved school, for example) five boys were with foster families; and two boys and two girls were living with relatives such as grandparents.

Looking back to their younger days, most people described their relationship with their mothers as 'good' (47.5 per cent of women; 53.7 per cent of men) or even 'excellent' (33.6 per cent of women; 32.5 per cent of men). Only ten women (4.2 per cent) and nine men (3.7 per cent) said their relationship with their mother had been 'poor' or 'terrible'. These included two men who had spent part of their adolescence in institutions. Poor relationships with fathers were more prevalent than those with mothers among the men (twenty-two, or 8.9 per cent); among the women only marginally so (5.9 per cent). Again, among the men it is notable that those living in institutions at the age of fifteen were particu-larly likely to describe their relationships with their fathers as poor (three out of six).

The age at which male respondents left home shows little rela-tionship to feelings about parents in childhood/adolescence. If we leave out of account the two men discussed above, then 60 per cent of those reporting earlier relationships with their fathers as 'poor' or even 'terrible' had nevertheless remained at home until they were over twenty years of age (compared with 64 per cent of those with better relationships). Similarly, apart from the two people institutionalized, all of the men reporting bad relationships with their mothers stayed in the family home until they were at least eighteen and 74 per cent until they were twenty.

Among the women, those who said their relationships with their parents were good were marginally more likely to stay at home until they were at least twenty (42 per cent of those whose relationship with their mothers was good compared with 38 per cent of the 'mixed' and 30 per cent of the 'poor'; 52 per cent of those whose relationship with their fathers was 'good' compared with 39 per cent of those whose relationship was 'mixed' and 43 per cent of those with 'poor').

The very small number of people who had lost their mothers (three boys, one girl) before they left school all left home early (before they were eighteen). Girls who had lost their fathers were also rather more likely to leave home early (three out of the six concerned left home before they were eighteen) but this was not true of the fatherless boys where only one did so (approximately the same proportion as among those with fathers).

If we look at *reasons* for leaving home early we find that about a fifth of those in each sex who left home before the age of eighteen did so because of factors relating to a more general break-up in the family (for example, parental split-up, introduction of a step-parent, family tensions, death, or illness). The main reason for early departure by women, however, was undoubtedly marriage (61 per cent) and, for men, continuing education or taking up work elsewhere (35 per cent). Conversely only two men said they left home to get married before they were eighteen and only a relatively few women (14 per cent) because of the demands of work or education.

If we relate age at leaving home to the extent of deviating behaviour reported by parents when our respondents were nine years old (see *Table 29*) there was no evidence that those with the highest scores (six or more) were likely to leave home early – in fact, among the men, the opposite was true. Indeed, in each sex, the most interesting group were those with four or five deviant items marked by their parents as, among those whose deviant scores were known, these were the people who were both most likely to *leave* home before the age of eighteen and most likely to *remain* at home into their late twenties. It is worth noting,

Table 29   *Age of leaving home by deviation score (parents) at nine years (cumulative frequencies)*

age left home	deviation score					
	0	1	2–3	4–5	6+	not known
females						
before 18th birthday	14 (12.8)	7 (14.0)	5 (13.2)	5 (27.8)	1 (10.0)	5 (38.5)
before 20th birthday	56 (51.4)	19 (38.0)	19 (50.0)	9 (50.0)	5 (50.0)	7 (53.8)
before survey (at age 26)	102 (93.6)	47 (94.0)	36 (94.7)	15 (83.3)	10 (100.0)	13 (100.0)
still at home	7 (6.4)	3 (6.0)	2 (5.3)	3 (16.7)	– (–)	– (–)
total	109 (100.0)	50 (100.0)	38 (100.0)	18 (100.0)	10 (100.0)	13 (100.0)
males						
before 18th birthday	8 (7.9)	8 (14.5)	5 (9.6)	3 (18.7)	1 (10.0)	2 (16.7)
before 20th birthday	33 (32.7)	19 (34.5)	22 (42.3)	6 (37.5)	3 (30.0)	6 (50.0)
before survey (at age 26)	84 (83.2)	42 (76.4)	47 (85.4)	12 (75.0)	5 (50.0)	11 (91.7)
still at home	17 (16.8)	13 (23.6)	5 (9.6)	4 (25.0)	5 (50.0)	1 (8.3)
total	101 (100.0)	55 (100.0)	52 (100.0)	16 (100.0)	10 (100.0)	12 (100.0)

however, that the group who had no original parents' questionnaires once again showed atypical features in that they were the most likely to have left home and also tended to leave home rather earlier (especially the females).

MARRIAGE

By the time they were twenty-six, 87 per cent of the women and 61 per cent of the men had been married at least once. The marked sex difference can be accounted for by the tendency of women to marry earlier. Thus, while just over half the people of each sex (52 per cent of men; 54 per cent of women) married for the first time in their twenties, a third of the women (34 per cent) had been teen-age brides (compared with only 9 per cent of males).

At the time of the survey, four-fifths (80 per cent) of the women and nearly three-fifths of the men were participating in intact marriages (though not necessarily their first) while a further 5 per cent of women and 8 per cent of men were living in stable partner-ships outside marriage. Only 5 per cent of women and 2 per cent of men were living alone or with children or had returned to their parents because of marital breakdown.

Perhaps because they had married earlier, the women were marginally more likely to have gone through a divorce than the men (16 out of 208, or 7.7 per cent of those married at least once compared with 5 out of 153, or 3.3 per cent of men) but propor-tions 'separated' (women 9 out of 208, or 4.3 per cent; men 6 out of 153, or 4.6 per cent) were nearly equal. Only one person (a woman) had been widowed.

In view of the relative youth of our respondents, it might be expected that those first marriages which had broken up must have been of very short duration. In part, this appears true: of the twenty divorced or separated women where duration of first marriage could be ascertained nine (45 per cent) had parted from their first husband after less than three years of marriage. On the other hand, nearly as high a number (eight, or 40 per cent) had waited for five or more years (and half of those for more than seven years). As we have already seen, fewer men than women had been divorced. In part, this reflects the tendency for men to marry later but, on the basis of the few cases available, there was also some evidence that they were less likely to suffer a marriage break-down within the first two years of marriage (22 per cent).

The evidence of any relationship between a broken marriage and the extent of deviation described by parents at nine was not strong. Men who had married were more than twice as likely to have suffered a marriage break-up if their deviation score was two or more (12.5 per cent; 5.2 per cent of those with scores less than two). The numbers involved are, however, very small indeed and, among the women (if we exclude the one woman whose husband died) there was no relationship at all between deviation and a broken first marriage.

By no means all of those who had suffered a marriage disruption returned to a single life (or that of the single parent). Nine women (including the widow) and three men had remarried while twelve women and seven men had found a new partnership in a stable liaison. (These included some who were not yet legally available for remarrying as their first marriage, or that of their partner, was not yet dissolved.)

STABLE LIAISONS OUTSIDE MARRIAGE

In the late 1970s the picture of Britain (particularly southern Britain) presented in the popular press or on television might lead to expectations of comparatively large numbers of young people living with partners outside marriage. In fact, as we have seen, the great majority of women and well over half of the men in our survey were married. Stable liaisons involving a shared home were relatively uncommon (nineteen men; twelve women) and were more likely to involve those who had been married, particularly those separated but not yet legally free to remarry. This was particularly marked among the women where only five out of thirty single women (17 per cent) were living with a partner compared with three out of seven (43 per cent) of those 'separated' and four out of eighteen (22 per cent) of those divorced. As six out of eighteen (33 per cent) of those divorced had remarried, it might be that the separated cohabiting women and their partners were also intending, when free, to regularize the situation.

Among the men also only 17 per cent of those not yet married were cohabiting, of those divorced, 20 per cent, and of those separated, 29 per cent. Men who had been through a divorce seemed particularly likely to find another partner fairly quickly (or perhaps before parting with their wives) since three out of five had remarried and the other two had found a stable 'partner'. Conversely, of the eighteen divorced women, six had remarried, four were in stable cohabiting relationships and the remaining eight were either living alone, living alone with their children, or had returned to their parents' home.

CHILDREN

By the age of twenty-six more than half the women (54.6 per cent) and a third of the men (36.6 per cent) were living in households containing their own children or those of their spouse/partner. The lower proportion of men can be explained in two ways: by the later age at which men married and by the tendency for children of broken marriages to remain with their mother. If we look at the proportion of *married* respondents in each sex living in households containing children, the sex difference is much reduced so that 60.4 per cent of men with intact marriages had one or more children as compared with 64.2 per cent of women. Among those whose marriages had broken up, four women were bringing up their children as single parents, none of the men. This tendency is also reflected in the household composition of those living in stable relationships outside marriage where fifteen out of the nineteen men (78.9 per cent) lived in childless households and eight out of the twelve women (66.7 per cent).

Most of these children were still under school age. This can perhaps be best illustrated by looking at the age of eldest children and those whose siblings have not yet arrived (those who were 'only' children at the time of the survey). Of these 224 children, 129 were under five years of age (57.6 per cent). When we consider further that of those 129 children, 79 (61.2 per cent) had at least one younger sister or brother, it can be seen how young, on the whole, our respondents' families were. Many, indeed, had not yet completed their family. This becomes evident when we look at the proportion of 'only' children in terms of their age. Where the first child was under three years old (seventy-five cases) 'only' children predominated and only nine (12 per cent) had a younger sibling: among the three to five-year-olds, however, the proportion with a younger sister or brother had risen to 75.9 per cent and for those over five to 88.3 per cent.

As might be expected a woman's age at her first marriage was closely associated with the age of her first (or eldest) child. Of those married before they were twenty (eighty), 62.5 per cent had at least one child of school age (five or older) while only eight women (10 per cent) had not yet started their families. Among those married in their twenties (121) more than half (sixty-five) were still childless while only five (4.1 per cent) had a child of five or over and twenty (16.5 per cent) one aged three or four. This would seem to offer some support for the hypothesis that those marrying later wait rather longer before having their first child.

Age at marriage and patterns of childbearing also related closely to the mother's educational history in terms of the highest qualification gained (see *Table 30*).

Table 30 shows that those women who had undertaken the most training were marginally more likely still to be living a single life at the age of twenty-six. More interestingly, however, even when we take this difference into account, we still find a very pronounced trend showing that the least qualified were the most likely to have children – and indeed were twice as likely to have one or more children at the time of the survey. Of the group of women with degrees and other professional qualifications who were currently married, had been married, or were living in a stable relationship outside marriage, only 38 per cent had a child or children and, of those, all but four had only one child. This is in marked contrast to the other groups who were not only more likely to have started a family but, having done so, were much more likely to have had two or more children.

Table 30 *Marriage and parenthood by highest educational qualification gained (women respondents)*

	highest qualification			
	graduate or professional non-graduate	secretarial/ clerical	other requiring vocational training	none
total in group	44	40	35	119
(a) number married, divorced/separated or in stable relationship outside marriage	37	34	33	110
(as % of total group)	(84.1)	(85.0)	(94.3)	(92.4)
(b) number with children	14	17	19	81
(as % of those in group (a))	(37.8)	(50.0)	(57.5)	(73.6)
(c) number with one child only	10	6	9	28
(as % of those in group (b))	(71.4)	(35.3)	(47.4)	(34.6)

In the group as a whole, the spacing of children followed a very regular pattern. As *Table 31* shows, very few women had a second child before their first was less than three years old but, by the time they were five, most children had at least one sibling and one in four had two or three.

In view of this tendency for younger siblings to arrive as the eldest became more independent, it might be expected that the proportion of mothers working outside the home would remain small (that is their employment opportunities would be geared to the age of their *youngest* child rather than the first born). This was not the case, however. There was a marked division between the proportion working whose first child was less than five (sixteen out of seventy-five, or 21.3 per cent) and those where (s)he was of school age (thirty-one out of fifty-five, or 56.4 per cent).

Table 31   *Age of first child by presence of siblings (women respondents only)*

age of first child	number of younger children in household			
	none	*1*	*2*	*3*
less than one year (N = 10)	10 (100.0)	–	–	–
one but less than three (N = 32)	28 (87.5)	4 (12.5)	–	–
three but less than five (N = 33)	10 (30.3)	23 (69.7)	–	–
five or older (N = 55)	6 (10.9)	34 (61.8)	11 (20.0)	4 (7.3)

The number of women who were coping as single parents because of marital breakdown was small, encompassing only six people (see *Table 32*), but it is noteworthy that four of them were working and that three of these four had two children each while the other had one child.

In general (as *Table 32* shows), the arrival of the first baby rather than marriage provided the impetus for moving out of paid employment and into the role of full-time home-maker. Only six women without children had left their jobs and most (possibly all) of these were expecting a baby. Those who had children (as might be expected) were more likely to be working full-time on child-care and home-making than to be employed outside the home. Nevertheless as *Table 32* shows, a sizeable minority (about one in three) of those with a child or children did have paid jobs (full- or part-time). Furthermore, rather than the proportion of employed mothers decreasing as the size of the family grew, it rose, so that women with three or four children were more likely to have jobs than those with only one.

In considering the question of employment outside the home, it must however be remembered that our data described the situation at a particular point in time and there is evidence that some, at least, of the women moved in and out of employment as the family situation changed. For example, the reasons given for leaving jobs show that thirty-eight women had left on *more than one*

Table 32 *Women's employment by marital status and number of children*

marital state	children	employed (full-time or part-time)	not employed outside the home
married or cohabiting	none	72[1] (92.3)	6 (7.7)
	one	16 (30.8)	36 (69.2)
	two	21 (36.2)	37 (63.8)
	three or more	6 (42.8)	8 (57.1)
divorced or separated and not cohabiting	none	6 (100.0)	– (–)
	one or more	4 (66.7)	2 (33.3)
single	none	24[1] (100.0)	– (–)

Note: [1]Including one woman still in full-time education.

occasion because of pregnancy and of these five had left three times. As might be expected, those leaving more than once were more likely to have married early. Of those married before they were twenty, 27.5 per cent gave pregnancy as the reason for leaving two or more jobs compared with only 12.5 per cent of those marrying later. The complexity of this situation is, however, perhaps better illustrated by a case history.

Alexis B. attended a secondary modern school where she was, according to herself, a reasonably bright pupil but didn't like school and was glad to leave at fifteen. She started work as an office junior (which was what she wanted) but became pregnant and left after a year. After the baby was born she went to work in a factory and stayed there two and a half years until she got married (when she was nineteen). She remained at home for three years, having another baby when she was twenty. Her marriage ended when she was twenty-two and she moved in with another man (with whom she was still living at the time of the survey) and also returned to work in a factory. After a year she left to have her third child but, about a year after the birth, returned once again to factory work. Apart from contact with her workmates she did not like her job but did enjoy housework and child-care.

This case history would suggest that one reason for returning to work may well be financial. Often, however, it is suggested that work may be seen as an escape from the tedium of housework. This was not explored directly but respondents were asked, as part of the questions on how they viewed various aspects of their life, a series of questions on their feelings about various household and child-care tasks. They were also asked at the end of this sub-series of questions: 'In general, how would you say you felt about being a housewife?'

As *Table 33* shows, the answers were interesting in that they showed a much more positive orientation than might be expected in the light of media pronouncements. Only 9 women out of the 208 covered by *Table 33* felt 'mostly dissatisfied' or worse, while 93 (45 per cent) said they were 'delighted' or 'pleased' and a further 67 (32 per cent) were 'mostly satisfied'. We can also see that with the exception of mothers with two or more children, those who were employed enjoyed being housewives rather less than those who were not. Indeed, among the women who had a partner but no children, one in six felt that the question did not apply to them as they were not 'housewives'.

HOUSING

By the time they were twenty-six, as might be expected, most people had set up their own home. Among those who were married (or in stable relationships) only three people, all women, were still living in the parental home and these cases seemed to involve the 'taking over' of the house of a widowed parent rather than being forced to live there for lack of something better. Single people were more likely to stay with their parents but, even here, a sizeable minority had fled the nest.

As *Table 34* shows, single people who had left home and divorced people who had not returned home were most likely to be living in privately rented accommodation. Those who were married or living in stable partnerships were predominantly buying their own houses. It is evident, however, that the men who were married were more likely to be living in rented accommodation

Table 33 *How women feel about being a housewife in general by marital situation and number of children (excluding single women and divorced/separated without partner/children)*[1]

	not known or not applic- able	delighted/ pleased	mostly satisfied	mixed/ neutral	mostly dis- satisfied	unhappy/ terrible
married, cohabiting, and not employed						
no children (6)	–	3	2	1	–	–
	(–)	(50.0)	(33.3)	(16.7)	(–)	(–)
one child (36)	1	20	8	5	–	2
	(2.8)	(55.6)	(22.2)	(13.9)	(–)	(5.6)
two or more children (45)	–	21	17	5	1	1
	(–)	(46.7)	(37.8)	(11.1)	(2.2)	(2.2)
all with partner and full-time housewives (87)	1	44	27	11	1	3
	(1.1)	(50.6)	(31.0)	(12.6)	(1.1)	(3.4)
married, cohabiting, and employed or in f/t education						
no children (72)	12	25	22	10	3	–
	(16.7)	(37.7)	(30.6)	(13.9)	(4.2)	(–)
one child (16)	–	4	8	2	2	–
	(–)	(25.0)	(50.0)	(12.5)	(12.5)	(–)
two or more children (27)	–	16	9	2	–	–
	(–)	(59.3)	(33.3)	(7.4)	(–)	(–)
all with partner and outside employment/ education (115)	12	45	39	14	5	–
	(10.4)	(39.1)	(33.9)	(12.2)	(4.3)	(–)
divorced/separated and no new partner						
full-time housewife and children (2)	–	2	–	–	–	–
	(–)	(100.0)	(–)	(–)	(–)	(–)
working plus children (4)	1	2	1	–	–	–
	(25.0)	(50.0)	(25.0)	(–)	(–)	(–)
all divorced with children (6)	1	4	1	–	–	–
	(16.7)	(66.7)	(16.7)	(–)	(–)	(–)

Note: [1] These categories were excluded from the table because of the rather different connotations of 'housework' for those still living in the parental home, flat-sharing, etc. Relatively few were living as single house-holders.

Table 34 *Marital status by type of housing*

	males				females			
	married/ stable liaison (N=163)	divorced/ separated (N=6)	single (N=77)	total (N=246)	married/ stable liaison (N=202)	divorced/ separated (N=12)	single (N=24)	total (N=238)
living in parental home	– (–)	3 (50.0)	50 (64.9)	53 (21.5)	3 (1.5)	4 (33.3)	14 (58.3)	21 (8.8)
buying own house	81 (49.7)	1 (16.7)	6 (7.8)	88 (35.8)	124 (61.4)	1 (8.3)	2 (8.3)	127 (53.4)
renting house from local authority	44 (27.0)	– (–)	1 1(1.3)	45 (18.3)	52 (25.7)	3 (25.0)	1 (4.2)	56 (23.5)
other rented property	34 (20.9)	2 (33.3)	18 (23.4)	54 (22.0)	15 (7.4)	3 (25.0)	6 (25.0)	24 (10.1)
other or not known	4 (2.4)	– (–)	2 (2.6)	6 (2.4)	8 (4.0)	1 (8.3)	1 (4.2)	10 (4.2)

and rather less likely to be buying their own house than were the women. The difference might be taken to reflect the later marriage age of the men, that is the stage of family building had not yet reached the house purchase stage. This, however, is not supported by the data shown in *Table 36*. It was also the case that those who married earliest (both men and women) were least likely to be buying their own homes at the time of the survey. Thus, while two-thirds of men married in their twenties were house-owners, this was true of only 17 per cent of those married in their teens. Among the women the difference was not so extreme but still favoured those marrying later (69 per cent to 45 per cent). Those marrying early were more likely to be living in property rented from the local authority (62 per cent of men married under twenty; 42 per cent of women).

The main determinant of type of housing, however, as might be expected, lay in the socio-economic status of the family. This can be shown by looking at the most recent job of married male respondents. As *Table 35* shows, the proportion of home-owners declines steadily as socio-economic status drops while the proportion of those in local authority housing steadily rises. The difference in house ownership between the lower (routine) grades of white-collar workers and the skilled manual workers is particularly interesting in view of what has been said about the 'embourgeoisement' of the working class in recent years.

It was less easy to relate house ownership to the status of married women's jobs. As we have clearly seen in Chapter 3, women's jobs tended to 'bunch' much more than the men's and, furthermore, a large proportion of women were not employed at the time of the survey. Nevertheless, bearing these problems in mind, some association did emerge here also between house ownership and type of work so that 88 per cent of married women in the top socio-economic status group (professional and so on) and 80 per cent of the 'intermediate' category were living in their own house compared with 64 per cent of those in more routine white-collar work and 44 per cent of those with manual jobs. In this case, however, we must remember that the point at issue is

Table 35 Housing type by socio-economic status of most recent job (married men only)

type of housing	socio-economic status					
	professional managerial administrative	intermediate non-manual	routine non-manual/ minor supervisory	skilled manual	other manual	not known
	(N=33)	(N=26)	(N=23)	(N=54)	(N=20)	(N=7)
house owner	23 (69.7)	15 (57.7)	13 (56.5)	21 (38.9)	5 (25.0)	4 (57.1)
rented from local authority	1 (3.0)	4 (15.4)	5 (21.7)	21 (38.9)	11 (55.0)	2 (28.6)
other rented	8 (24.2)	6 (23.1)	5 (21.7)	10 (18.5)	4 (20.0)	1 (14.3)
not known: other	1 (3.0)	1 (3.8)	– (–)	2 (3.7)	– (–)	– (–)

Table 36 *Housing by size of family (excluding those still living with parents)*

	no children	1 child	2 children	3 or more children
females				
house owners	62 (48.8)	31 (24.4)	29 (22.8)	5 (3.9)
local authority tenants	9 (16.1)	14 (25.0)	23 (41.1)	10 (17.9)
other rented accommodation	7 (29.2)	8 (33.3)	9 (37.5)	– (–)
males				
house owners	53 (60.2)	20 (22.7)	14 (15.9)	1 (1.1)
local authority tenants	8 (17.8)	9 (20.0)	22 (48.9)	6 (13.3)
other rented accommodation	32 (59.2)	9 (16.7)	10 (18.5)	3 (5.6)

not merely the status of the woman's job but the fact that she, as well as her husband, is a wage-earner.

This hypothesis is reinforced by the data shown in *Table 36*. This shows that those who were house-owners (or whose spouses were) were markedly more likely to be childless than were those living in local authority housing. In part this may reflect public housing policy by which allocation of a house is influenced by the arrival of a baby, reducing the eligibility of childless couples. If this is so it should be reflected in a higher proportion of childless couples in other rented accommodation. This does not seem to be the case, if we make allowance for single people and divorced people living alone since these account for more than half of the childless people in private rented accommodation.

Most of our respondents were 'satisfied' (50 per cent of women; 58 per cent of men) or 'very satisfied' (37 per cent of women; 26 per cent of men) with their accommodation at the time of the survey. There was some internal variation, however, so that while only 6 per cent of women living in their own houses expressed some dissatisfaction, 16 per cent of men did so. Least satisfied in each sex were the local authority housing tenants (21 per cent of women; 24 per cent of men dissatisfied).

ECONOMIC WELL-BEING

Interestingly, despite mortgage demands, male respondents who were buying their own houses were markedly more likely to see themselves as 'well off' in relation to other people than were those in any other type of housing while men living in local authority housing were least likely to do so. As *Table 37* shows, among the women these differences were much less marked, with those still living at home the most positive about their economic situation.

For men, the acquisition of a spouse appears to result in a marked increase in economic well-being so that the proportion seeing themselves as 'well off' rises from 29 per cent of those living with their parents, living alone, or sharing flats, to 54 per cent of those with a partner but no children. The relationship is even more marked if we look at those seeing themselves as 'badly off'. This encompasses 32 per cent of men living alone, 15 per cent of those still living with their parents and only 6 per cent of childless couples (where 54 per cent felt 'well off'). With the arrival of children the situation deteriorates slightly and 17 per cent of men felt 'badly off'. Among the women, as we have already seen, the best time is before marriage, while they are living at home, but even among those living alone or in shared flats, for example, only 14 per cent felt 'badly off'. With the arrival of a partner this fell to 4 per cent (but only 34 per cent felt 'well off') before again rising (to 13 per cent) with the arrival of children.

Indeed it appears to be the arrival of the *first* child which produces the strain so that while 18 per cent of men with one child felt 'badly off', this rose only to 21 per cent of those with larger

Table 37   *Percentage of each housing type describing themselves as 'well off'*

	living with parents	own house	local authority tenant	other rented	other/ not known
females	38.1	32.3	23.6	29.2	10.0
males	28.8	45.5	17.7	24.5	20.0

families. For the women the proportion remained at 17 per cent in each case.

A broken marriage, however, had a very deleterious effect. Of those in each sex who were separated or divorced and had not yet found a new partner, half said they were 'badly off'. In the worst position of all were those whose marriages had broken leaving them as single parents, *all* of whom said they were 'badly off'.

— 5

HEALTH

DEATHS

By 1977 five of our original group were dead. As might be expected in this age-group, accidents accounted for three of the male deaths while the fourth was attributed to cancer. The only girl to die had done so at eighteen just before going to college. It is possible that some of those not found were also dead but we would have expected (albeit rather optimistically) that this would have emerged as a result of our NHS tracing of the 'missing' cases.

HOSPITALIZATION

Between 1961 and 1977 43.5 per cent of our male respondents and 77.3 per cent of our females had spent at least one night in hospital. The large sex difference is, of course, due to the almost universal practice of women being admitted to hospital for the birth of their babies (though two of our respondents, living abroad, had apparently had their babies at home). 'Normal' childbirth (that is not involving surgical intervention, prolonged hospitalization, or other noted complications) was *a* cause of hospitalization for 109 women (45.8 per cent) and the *only* cause for 52 (21.8 per cent). Complications of pregnancy or childbirth were mentioned by thirty-two (13.4 per cent) and diseases of the genito-urinary system by twenty-six women (10.9 per cent). The other most common reasons for women being admitted to hospital were, in order of importance, diseases of the digestive system (forty-seven, or 19.7 per cent), diseases of the respiratory system (twenty-four, or 10.1 per cent) and fractures, lacerations, and so on (fourteen, or 5.9 per cent). Using the RCGP classification system, only a few cases emerged in any other single category, such as five women with neoplasms, four poisonings, two with diseases of the nervous system. Not one woman said she had been admitted for psychiatric reasons.

Among the men, accidents involving fractures and lacerations were the main cause of admission (forty-four, or 17.9 per cent of the male respondents; 41.5 per cent of those with one or more admissions). As with the women, this was followed by diseases of the digestive system (thirty-six, or 16.6 per cent) and of the respiratory system (fifteen, or 6.1 per cent). Diseases of the genito-urinary system, however, were of fairly minimal importance among the men (five, or 2 per cent) while those affecting the muscular-skeletal system and connective tissues were more frequent (twelve, or 4.9 per cent compared with six, or 2.5 per cent of women). Only three men said they had been admitted because of mental disorders and similarly small numbers occurred under other classifications.

As *Table 38* shows, if we exclude normal childbirth the distribution of hospital admissions is remarkably similar in each case with more than half of those admitted having been patients on one occasion only while relatively few people had more than two admissions.

Table 38   *Total number of hospital admissions by sex*

number of admissions	males	females	females excluding those admitted for normal childbirth only
one	60 (56.1)	60 (32.6)	71 (54.6)
two	29 (27.1)	64 (34.8)	35 (26.9)
three	9 (8.4)	36 (19.6)	14 (10.8)
four or more	9 (8.4)	24 (13.0)	9 (6.9)
number not known	–	–	1 (0.8)
total with admissions	107	184	130
percentage of total group	(43.4)	(77.3)	(54.6)

It might be expected that multiple admissions would relate to some particular weakness in the individual concerned, that is the *cause* would be the same for each admission. This was true only to a limited extent. If we exclude normal childbirth (where sixty-one women reported two or more admissions) we find that repeated admissions for the same cause occur mainly in single cases. Among the women the exceptions were diseases of the genito-urinary system (six), complications of pregnancy and childbirth (four), and diseases of the digestive system (three). Among the men, fractures and lacerations were the only causes of hospitalization for 40 per cent of those admitted more than once and 50 per cent of those with at least three admissions. The only other categories in which multiple admissions for the same cause were reported by more than one man were diseases of the digestive system (four) and of the skeleto-muscular system (two).

In terms of demand for hospital in-patient facilities, we find that 12.2 per cent of women and 9.8 per cent of men had occupied a hospital bed for a total (over *all* their admissions) of four weeks or more during the sixteen years of the inter-survey period. Since total duration reflects the number of admissions as well as the severity of any one admission, the health experience of individuals may, however, be better illustrated by looking at the length of the *longest* single period spent in hospital. This shows that only 8.4 per cent of women and 6.5 per cent of men had spent at least one period of four weeks or more in hospital. Of those with one or more admissions, quite a substantial minority (30 per cent of men; 31 per cent of women) had never spent a consecutive period of more than six days in hospital. Only one person (a male psychiatric patient) had spent more than a year there. He had been admitted for three such long periods and was, in fact, in hospital when interviewed.

OPERATIONS

Most men admitted to hospital had undergone surgery (70.1 per cent) and the same was true of women entering hospital at least once for reasons other than a normal confinement (76.7 per cent).

The main cause of surgical intervention for men was accidental injury (as might be expected from the causes for admission) so that 20 per cent of those undergoing operations did so at least once for this reason. The other most prevalent procedure was removal of the appendix (6 per cent of all men; 20 per cent of those with operations). Among the women appendectomy was also among the most common operations (6.3 per cent of all women; 15.2 per cent of those undergoing any surgery) but was marginally exceeded by dental operations (6.7 per cent of all women; 16.2 per cent of those with operations). Other types of operation were relatively rare (for example D and C, 3.4 per cent; other genitourinary intervention, 2.5 per cent; caesarians, 2 per cent).

OUT-PATIENT TREATMENT

In contrast to the picture among in-patients, men were more likely than women to seek out-patient treatment so that three-quarters

(75.6 per cent) of our male respondents had visited hospital out-patient facilities (including casualty but not attendance for routine examinations or prophylactic purposes such as mass X-ray, or, in the case of women, routine antenatal classes, examinations, and so on) compared with only just over half (53.4 per cent) of the women. Furthermore, the men were more likely to return as out-patients on different occasions for *different* complaints so that while only nineteen women (8 per cent) cited three or more separate causes for out-patient treatment, fifty-nine men (24 per cent) did so. The sex difference remains substantial even when allowance is made for the smaller proportion of women obtaining *any* out-patient treatment so that the ratio of male out-patients treated for at least three complaints (31.7 per cent of male out-patients) to female (15 per cent of female out-patients) was still two to one.

In terms of actual hospital time consumed – as measured by number of visits – the men as a whole had clearly made more use of out-patient facilities than the women so that the average number of visits per head (including those who had never been out-patients) was 4.14 compared with 2.75 for the female respondents. Much of this difference, however, is due to the smaller proportion of men with no out-patient treatment at all. If we look only at those of each sex who actually attended as out-patients, the number of visits per attender averages out at 5.21 for women as compared with 5.62 for men.

As might be expected the major cause of male attendance at casualty/out-patient clinics was broken bones and sprains, with more than half of our male respondents (51.6 per cent) having attended at least once for such a reason but only 19.7 per cent of the female. The only other types of problems to be cited by ten or more men involved, in order of frequency, the muscular-skeletal system (twenty-seven), the respiratory system (sixteen), skin (fifteen), eyes (thirteen), the digestive system (twelve), and burns (ten). The list for women contained four of the same items, that is skin (twenty-one), the respiratory (sixteen), digestive (fifteen), and muscular-skeletal systems (fourteen). Additionally, however, as with in-patient treatment, problems of the genito-urinary system assumed some importance (nineteen). Psychiatric out-patient treatment was mentioned by only eight people – four men and four women.

Because of the very great contribution made by fractures, lacerations, bruises, and so on to the use made of hospital facilities – particularly out-patient ones – by male respondents, a special study was made of accidental injury among the men. This is described in Chapter 6.

GP CONSULTATIONS

Only about one in four of informants (29 per cent of men; 23 per cent of women) said they had consulted their family practitioner about 'persistent, serious, or worrying problems'. The reasons for such consultations varied with psychiatric problems taking the lead among the women (thirteen cases) followed by allergies (eight), gastro-intestinal complaints (seven), and muscular pains, backache, and so one (five). The same problems occurred most frequently among the men but in slightly different order so that gastro-intestinal complaints (ten) and allergies (ten) were most frequently cited while psychiatric symptoms fell to joint third place (six cases) with muscular and back pains.

PSYCHIATRIC PROBLEMS

As has been shown already, very few people said that they had received treatment for psychiatric problems: three men had been in-patients; four of each sex had received out-patient treatment in hospitals, and thirteen women and six men had been treated by their family practitioners. These figures raise two questions: first, are these separate categories or do the same people reappear under different headings, and second, are the small numbers in each category a result of those suffering from psychiatric problems being less likely to respond, especially to postal questionnaires?

So far as overlap of categories is concerned, none of the three male in-patients mentioned either discussing the problem with their general practitioner or receiving out-patient treatment. (There were no females with psychiatric admissions.) Out-patient treatment did overlap slightly with treatment by general practitioners but by only a small amount so that only two of the six men who consulted their doctors about psychiatric symptoms, and one of the thirteen women, had also received psychiatric out-patient treatment at hospital. Looked at from another viewpoint, only two out of four of those receiving out-patient treatment in each sex indicated any substantial involvement of their family doctor.

Taking into account the small overlap that did exist, the total number of people who had received or were receiving some psychiatric treatment, then, amounted to eleven men (4.5 per cent) and sixteen women (6.7 per cent).

Does this reflect differential response? This is difficult to answer. A check was carried out on 'missing' cases using the records system of the psychiatric hospital covering most of the Buckinghamshire area. This in fact produced one of our in-patients who was then interviewed. None of the other missing people appeared. This does not mean that they were free of psychiatric problems – merely that they had not been admitted to *that* hospital and issues of confidentiality as well as practicability meant that wider searches were virtually impossible. The same was even more true of out-patients (where psychiatric records were not kept separately) and family doctor consultations. Bearing in mind that our 'missing' cases were those who could not be traced locally the problem was insurmountable.

So far as our respondents are concerned, self-perceptions of psychiatric malaise (in answer to the question 'Have you ever felt that you might suffer some form of nervous breakdown?') had affected more people than might be suggested by the small proportion receiving treatment so that twenty-nine men (11.8 per cent) and forty-eight women (20.2 per cent) reported at least one such occasion, mostly in adult life (that is over the age of eighteen) rather than adolescence (only four men and eleven women).

Those answering positively included, among the men, two out of the three people who had been admitted to hospital for psychiatric problems (the third did not answer the question, perhaps feeling that 'nervous breakdown' was an inadequate synonym for chronic schizophrenia) and three out of the four treated as outpatients. Among the women, all four out-patients were covered. In each sex, people who felt they had been at risk of a 'nervous breakdown' were more likely to have been treated for a 'persistent or worrying health problem' of some kind (not necessarily psychiatric) by their family doctor (65.2 per cent compared with 25.6 per cent of others among the men; 52.1 per cent compared with 15.9 per cent of breakdown-free among the women). As we have already seen, the number of people treated by general practitioners for psychiatric problems was small (six men, thirteen women) so that while most of those receiving psychiatric help (five men, nine women) felt they had been threatened by a breakdown, the reverse was not true and only a minority of those fearing a breakdown said they had received treatment from their doctor (17.2 per cent of men at risk; 18.8 per cent of women). These proportions are, however, much higher than those occurring in the rest of our sample (0.5 per cent for men; 2.1 per cent for women). Those saying they were affected in adolescence only were less likely to mention treatment by their family doctor for psychiatric problems (none of the three men and only one of the ten women) than those with adult manifestations (five out of twenty-six men; eight out of thirty-eight women). This may reflect a tendency to record only relatively recent consultations rather than less likelihood of seeking advice at a younger age. The numbers of those mentioning problems in adolescence are, in any case, too small to make valid inferences.

HEALTH AT TWENTY-SIX

Respondents were asked whether or not they had been bothered by various 'complaints' in the previous few weeks and whether they felt this had affected them 'a little' or 'quite a lot'. The list of complaints and their frequencies is shown in *Table 39*. As can be seen, the picture is remarkably similar in each sex (with the only statistically significant sex differences occurring in the cases of dizziness and headaches – both more common among women).

Among the men, few problems (apart from colds and flu) affected more than a minority of respondents. Only 'general aches and pains', headaches, upset stomach, back pain, and feeling generally run-down each affected as many as one in four; palpitations and dizziness only one in twenty.

Among the women about half said they suffered from symptoms of pre-menstrual tension (PMT) and only marginally fewer complained of headaches, while other relatively frequent complaints involved (in order of frequency) colds or flu, general aches and pains, feeling generally run-down, nervousness or tension, back pains, and stomach upsets.

How do these various 'complaints' interrelate? Two possible questions must be considered: first, do the same people tend to reappear as having different symptoms, and second, if so are they symptomatic of one particular problem? Dealing with the second question first, one obvious possibility was that those who had suffered from 'flu-ish' colds were reporting various difficulties which had occurred only *because* of the flu, for example aches and pains, headaches, feeling generally run-down. Comparing those who reported such problems and who had had colds or flu with those who hadn't, however, revealed almost identical distributions. The only items showing even marginal differences were 'general aches and pains' (women: 35.2 per cent of those with colds, 26.5 per cent of those without; men: 38.6 per cent compared with 33.3 per cent); headaches (women: 50.5 per cent of those with colds, 46.1 per cent of those without; men: 31.7 per cent compared with 25.5 per cent); run-down (36.3 per cent of women with colds, 25.2 of those without; men: 24.8 per cent in each case).

Problems did not necessarily come singly however. If we exclude 'colds and flu' we still find that half of those who had ticked one item had also ticked at least two others (49.5 per cent of

Table 39 *Recently experienced health problems by intensity and sex*

problem	females			males		
	not experi- enced	yes: a little trouble	yes: a lot of trouble	not experi- enced	yes: a little trouble	yes: a lot of trouble
colds or flu	147 (61.8)	61 (25.6)	30 (12.6)	145 (58.9)	80 (32.5)	21 (8.5)
dizziness	209 (87.8)	23 (9.7)	6 (2.5)	233 (94.7)	12 (4.9)	1 (0.4)
general aches and pains	167 (70.2)	58 (24.4)	13 (5.5)	169 (68.7)	63 (25.6)	14 (5.7)
headaches	126 (52.9)	84 (35.3)	28 (11.8)	173 (70.3)	67 (27.2)	6 (2.4)
nervousness/ tension	168 (70.6)	56 (23.5)	14 (5.9)	194 (78.9)	43 (17.5)	9 (3.7)
rapid heart beat	228 (95.8)	8 (3.4)	2 (0.8)	230 (93.5)	15 (6.1)	1 (0.4)
shortness of breath	223 (93.7)	14 (5.9)	1 (0.4)	218 (88.6)	24 (9.8)	4 (1.6)
skin rash	198 (83.2)	30 (12.6)	10 (4.2)	217 (88.2)	25 (10.2)	5 (2.0)
upset stomach	177 (74.4)	52 (21.8)	9 (3.8)	173 (70.3)	61 (24.8)	12 (4.9)
back pain	172 (72.6)	54 (22.8)	11 (4.6)	180 (73.2)	54 (22.0)	12 (4.9)
difficulty in getting to sleep	184 (77.3)	39 (16.4)	15 (6.3)	206 (83.7)	33 (13.5)	7 (2.8)
waking early and unable to get back to sleep	207 (87.0)	22 (9.2)	9 (3.8)	217 (88.2)	24 (9.8)	5 (2.0)
feeling generally run-down	168 (70.6)	58 (24.4)	12 (5.0)	185 (75.2)	52 (21.1)	9 (3.7)
period pains	144 (60.8)	68 (28.7)	24 (10.1)	–	–	–
heavy bleeding	185 (78.4)	21 (8.9)	29 (12.3)	–	–	–
feeling irritable, tense, or tearful just before period	113 (47.7)	84 (35.4)	39 (16.5)	–	–	–

men with one or more complaints; 50.5 per cent of women) while nearly one in ten of the women who had complaints had marked at least seven (9.4 per cent compared with 3.5 per cent of men) of the twelve possibilities open to both sexes (that is excluding the three items relating to menstruation).

As can be seen from *Table 39* most of these problems were reported to cause only 'a little trouble'. 'A lot' of trouble caused by one or more complaints was, however, indicated by sixty-eight women (28.6 per cent of informants) and fifty-two men (21.1 per cent). Of this group, the majority in each sex (57.7 per cent of

Table 40   *Menstrual problems by intensity of other health problems*

problem	trouble caused	total health complaints ticked (excluding colds)					
		none	1 or 2 'a little'	3 or more 'a little'	1 'a lot'	2 or more 'a lot'	total
period pains	none	26 (72.2)	51 (65.4)	38 (67.9)	16 (43.2)	15 (48.4)	146 (61.3)
	'a little'	9 (25.0)	19 (24.4)	15 (26.8)	14 (37.8)	11 (35.5)	68 (28.6)
	'a lot'	1 (2.8)	8 (10.3)	3 (5.4)	7 (18.9)	5 (16.1)	24 (10.1)
heavy bleeding	none	29 (80.5)	69 (88.5)	46 (82.1)	26 (70.3)	18 (58.1)	188 (79.0)
	'a little'	5 (13.9)	4 (5.1)	6 (10.7)	3 (8.1)	3 (9.7)	21 (8.8)
	'a lot'	2 (5.6)	5 (6.4)	4 (7.1)	8 (21.6)	10 (32.3)	29 (12.2)
PMT	none	27 (75.0)	37 (47.4)	23 (41.1)	18 (48.6)	10 (32.3)	15 (48.3)
	'a little'	9 (25.0)	33 (42.3)	26 (46.4)	10 (27.0)	6 (19.4)	84 (35.3)
	'a lot'	– (–)	8 (10.3)	7 (12.5)	9 (24.3)	15 (48.4)	39 (16.4)
total		36	78	56	37	31	238

men; 54.4 per cent of women) reported only *one* major problem on its own or, more commonly, accompanied by minor ones. Between three and five complaints had, however, caused 'a lot' of trouble to six men and eleven women while three women had been affected markedly by six of the items on the list. On the whole, then, the women seemed more likely not only to have multiple problems but also to have more 'trouble' with them even if we exclude the specifically female complaints.

As *Table 40* shows, however, those women who experienced 'a lot of bother' with some of the health problems listed (excluding colds and flu) were also markedly more likely to have 'a lot' of trouble with at least one type of menstrual problem. Indeed, if we combine these categories and relate 'a lot of bother' with *any* of the three 'female' complaints to 'a lot' of trouble with the other health items, the relationship becomes even more marked. Thus, of those women experiencing 'a lot' of trouble with any *one* or more of the items on the general health list, more than half (54.4 per cent) also had 'a lot of trouble' with at least one aspect of menstruation; for those experiencing no more than 'a little' trouble on any health item, the proportion fell to 16.4 per cent; and for those with no health problems to 8.3 per cent.

Looked at in more detail, it appeared that complaints of premenstrual tension were those most closely related to 'a lot' of trouble with other health problems. As *Table 39* shows, the number of women having 'a lot' of trouble with any specific type of complaint was small. If, however, we look at those items where at least 5 per cent of women were affected (see *Table 41*) we can see that the proportion also complaining of much trouble with menstruation was in nearly every case more than twice that found in the total sample. Only in the case of pre-menstrual tension, however, does the proportion rise threefold in all items except difficulty in falling asleep. Thus nearly three-quarters of those suffering 'a lot' from nerves/tension also specifically mentioned 'a lot' of trouble with PMT as did at least half of those who felt rundown or suffered 'a lot' from general aches and pains and/or headaches.

Table 41   *Health problems where 'a lot' of trouble was reported by at least 5 per cent of women by 'a lot' of problems with menstruation*

health problem	number having 'a lot' of trouble	number (percentage) having 'a lot' of trouble with		
		period pains	heavy bleeding	PMT
headaches	28	6	7	14
	(100.0)	(21.4)	(24.1)	(50.0)
difficulty getting to sleep	15	1	3	5
	(100.0)	(6.7)	(20.0)	(33.3)
nerves	14	3	4	9
	(100.0)	(21.4)	(28.6)	(64.3)
general aches and pains	13	3	4	7
	(100.0)	(23.1)	(30.8)	(53.8)
feeling run-down	12	3	6	7
	(100.0)	(25.0)	(50.0)	(58.3)
all women	238	24	29	39
	(100.0)	(10.1)	(12.2)	(16.4)

Despite these problems women were *not* more likely to be incapacitated by their ailments, however. Asked if, during the previous six months, illness or injury had led to time off work or 'carrying out your usual activities' 45.7 per cent of men said 'yes' compared with only 36.6 per cent of women. In the main this reflected a greater tendency for the men to take a few days off as the proportion absent for at least seven days was the same (12 per cent) in each sex.

One possible reason may be that housewives (married or divorced women not working outside the home) were almost twice as likely as single working women to have experienced a health problem (excluding the menstrual ones) causing 'a lot' of trouble (32.6 per cent; 16.7 per cent of single; 28.0 per cent of married/divorced women who were employed). These housewives may have been least able to take time off from their 'usual duties' even if feeling unfit.

CONSUMPTION OF MEDICINES

As *Table 42* shows, about one in three of male informants said that they had taken some kind of medicine or tablets 'during the last few weeks' (or were still taking them) but among the women the proportion was much higher. In each case, however, the vast majority (more than 80 per cent) of those who had taken some form of medication had taken only one type. Only twelve men and twenty-five women had taken as many as three or four. The remedy most frequently resorted to comprised aspirin, para-cetamol, and other pain relievers which tended to be self-pre-scribed.

Relatively few people had taken sleeping pills, tranquillizers, and other medication for 'nerves' though, in each case – as indeed, with the other categories – women were more likely to have been affected than were men. Women were also more likely to have received a prescription from their family doctor (64.5 per cent of those taking some form of medication compared with 50 per cent of men).

SMOKING AND DRINKING

Fewer than half of our informants were current smokers (48.3 per cent of men; 36.3 per cent of women); 14.0 per cent of men and 15.7 per cent of women had smoked at some time and given up. This shows that women were rather less likely to smoke at all but, among those who did, the proportion of those who smoked 'frequently' was nearly identical in each sex (approximately three out of every four).

In drinking habits (as admitted) also there was a pronounced sex difference. As *Table 43* shows, nearly half of the men said they drank 'often' whereas only about one in six of the women described themselves in this way. Conversely 21 per cent of women said they never or 'practically never' drank alcohol compared with only 9 per cent of men. We cannot, of course, say whether these

Table 42 *Medicines consumed recently by reason and source*

reason	source: males			source: females		
	none	GP prescription	prescribed by self/ chemist	none	GP prescription	prescribed by self/ chemist
to help you sleep	242 (98.4)	4 (1.6)	–	228 (95.8)	8 (3.4)	2 (0.8)
as a tonic	234 (95.1)	2 (0.8)	10 (4.1)	221 (92.9)	14 (5.9)	3 (1.3)
for your nerves	243 (98.8)	3 (1.2)	–	227 (95.4)	11 (4.6)	–
to relieve pain	204 (82.9)	16 (6.5)	26 (10.6)	178 (74.8)	13 (5.5)	47 (19.7)
for any other reason	218 (88.6)	17 (6.9)	11 (4.5)	171 (71.8)	54 (22.7)	
total receiving medication	168 (68.3)	39 (15.9)	39 (15.9)	100 (42.0)	89 (37.4)	49 (20.6)

Table 43 *Frequency of drinking*

	never	practically never	occasionally	often
males	10 (2.0)	36 (7.1)	219 (43.2)	242 (47.7)
females	20 (4.0)	84 (16.9)	304 (61.3)	88 (17.7)

answers reflect 'real' drinking habits or whether they are coloured by what informants saw as sex-appropriate behaviour.

RELATIONSHIP BETWEEN HEALTH PROBLEMS
REPORTED BY PARENTS IN 1961 AND
SUBSEQUENT USE OF NHS

In the 1961 study parents were asked to indicate whether or not their children had suffered from a comprehensive selection of health problems ranging from travel sickness and frequent colds to more serious or persistent problems such as eczema, asthma, heart trouble, and so on.

Relating each of these ailments to subsequent use of hospital facilities revealed very little. One possible reason lies in the very small number of children who were said to suffer from the more serious problems. For example, no children had been diagnosed as diabetic by the age of nine; only one boy was spastic; only one person of each sex had a heart problem. Even where numbers were sufficient for meaningful analysis, however, very little emerged apart from the outstanding health of males, seen by their parents as 'too fat' in 1961, who were significantly less likely to be admitted to hospital, to have operations, or even to attend out-patient clinics. A similar (but less marked) situation existed among their female counterparts. It may well be that trouble would emerge later but certainly up to the age of twenty-six these were the healthiest group!

No single type of health problem at nine years of age related to increased use of health facilities later. Adding up the total number of health problems reported by parents, however, there was evidence, among the men, that those people whose mothers had ticked four or more 'problems' in 1961 were more likely to have been admitted to hospital later (12 out of 17, or 70.6 per cent, compared with 88 out of 217, or 40.6 per cent of rest) and more likely to undergo operations (9 out of 17, or 52.9 per cent, compared with 59 out of 216, or 27.3 per cent of rest) but not any more likely to attend out-patient clinics (12 out of 17, or 70.6 per cent, compared with 157 out of 211, or 74.4 per cent of rest). Among female respondents there was no association between number of items ticked in 1961 and involvement in either in-patient (excluding normal confinement) or out-patient treatment.

To provide a different approach, we also had information provided by parents or hospital admissions up to 1961. This showed that 106 of our male respondents (43.1 per cent) and 83 women (34.9 per cent) had been in hospital at least once by the age of nine. Most of these admissions had occurred after the child reached school age, with seventy-five boys and fifty-eight girls entering hospital between the ages of five and nine years, mostly (54.5 per cent of boys; 65.5 per cent of girls) to undergo the removal of their tonsils and/or adenoids. This was also the main single reason for admission among those aged between one and four when they were admitted. This group was smaller, comprising only twenty-five girls and thirty-four boys, but of these twelve girls and thirteen boys had their tonsils/adenoids removed.

Relatively few people (six girls and fourteen boys) had been admitted to hospital during their first year or kept in because of problems noticed at, or associated with, their birth. Of these three boys and one girl required surgical intervention for a condition they were born with but, in other cases, reasons for early hospitalization varied and no particular pattern could be discerned. Children admitted during their first year did, however, spend rather more time in hospital so that more than half the boys (eight out of fourteen) and all six girls spent more than a week there compared with 40 per cent of girls and 47 per cent of boys who went into hospital between the ages of one and four.

Early hospitalization appeared to have little relationship to later health. Indeed comparing those who had been admitted (i) between birth and their first birthday, and (ii) between their first and fifth birthdays, with those who had not, we found that, among the *men*, a practically identical picture emerged at follow-up with respect to the proportions undergoing operations, proportions attending out-patient clinics (and proportions attending more than eight times) and the proportion experiencing one or more health problems at the age of twenty-six. For the men, then, early hospitalization did not help predict later use of health service facilities or an increased likelihood of experiencing even minor health problems by the age of twenty-six.

Among the women, the very small number admitted during their first year (six) makes analysis difficult and possibly unreliable. But, for what it is worth, there was no indication that those in hospital before the age of one were more likely to suffer from later health problems. Those women who had been in-patients between their first and fifth birthdays, however, were slightly more likely to have attended out-patient clinics (and to have attended on eight or more occasions). They were also more likely to have at least one health problem causing them 'a lot' of trouble at the age of twenty-six.

HEALTH PROBLEMS AT NINE AND AT TWENTY-SIX

Although no association was found between use of health service facilities and individual health problems at the age of nine, it seemed worth investigating whether certain types of health problem, such as a tendency to be nervous, to have headaches, and so on, might make their appearance in childhood. It was decided, therefore, to look at those people whose parents had described them at nine years of age as highly strung or as suffering from headaches or stomach-aches once a month or more often and to see whether similar tendencies were still apparent when they were twenty-six.

In neither sex were those described by their parents as 'highly strung' children more likely to see themselves as having 'a lot' of trouble with nervousness/tenseness when they were twenty-six though the women who had been so classified were marginally more likely to see themselves as having 'a little' trouble (32.5 per cent to 23.2 per cent). 'Highly strung' girls *were*, however, much more likely to experience 'a lot' of trouble with pre-menstrual tension (30.0 per cent compared with 13.5 per cent of others); the proportions having 'a little' trouble showed no variation.

Headaches definitely persisted. Of men suffering from headaches at least once a month as nine-year-olds, a third (33.3 per cent) were still having some trouble (either 'a lot' or 'a little') at twenty-six (compared with 22 per cent of those free from headaches as children). Among the women the relationship was even more marked with 27.6 per cent of those who had headaches as children having 'a lot' of trouble with headaches as adults compared with only 6.5 per cent of those who had none earlier. There was also a relationship to pre-menstrual tension so that 31 per cent of those with frequent headaches at nine complained of 'a lot' of trouble compared with 13 per cent of those without any.

Only fourteen men were said by their parents to be suffering from stomach-ache at least once a month at nine years of age but, of these, six (42.9 per cent) were still experiencing problems at twenty-six. Among those without any reported pain in childhood the proportion fell to 29 per cent and, among those with more occasional manifestations, was even lower (23 per cent). More women had been affected in childhood (twenty-five) but they were only marginally more likely to report pains as adults (32 per cent of those with frequent pains were still affected compared with 25 per cent of the others). There was, however, among the women (but not the men) some relationship between 'tummy pains' in childhood and nervousness/tenseness in adult life so that 40 per cent of those with frequent pains said they now had some trouble of this kind (mainly 'a little') compared with 27.9 per cent of those less affected as children. They were also rather more likely to suffer from 'a lot' of trouble (but not 'a little') with both pre-menstrual tension (24 per cent of those with frequent stomach-ache compared with 14 per cent of others) and period pains (20 per cent compared with 8.4 per cent of the rest).

BEHAVIOUR AT NINE YEARS OLD AND
SUBSEQUENT HEALTH

There was no evidence of a straightforward linear relationship between the extent of deviation (measured in terms of the total number of deviating traits indicated by parents) at nine years of age and subsequent ill health as measured in terms either of use of health facilities or of current health problems reported by respondents themselves at twenty-six. Indeed, as *Table 44* shows, the distribution was often U-shaped with those with middling scores being the most likely to have made use of health services. Those with the highest deviation scores (six or more) were among the least likely to have occupied a hospital bed for reasons other than normal delivery, to have consulted their family doctor on some major matter or, if female, to have visited an out-patient department. (Among the men the very deviant were most likely to have been out-patients but not to have paid a lot of visits.)

So far as self-reported 'problems' of health at the age of twenty-six were concerned, *absence* of such problems followed a U-distribution among the women so that those least likely to have any problems occurred at the extremes of deviation, that is those with *no* behaviour problems at nine and those with a lot. Among the men no clear pattern emerges but those with no deviating traits, or only one, at nine were more likely to have four or more current health problems than were those who had been more problematic children.

Since the lack of association shown in *Table 44* might be influenced by the grouping together of people with different kinds of behaviour at nine – and therefore, possibly, different health experiences – it was felt useful also to look at individual types of behaviour in more detail.

Table 44 Total number of deviating behaviour traits reported by parents in 1961 by subsequent use of health service and state at age of twenty-six (percentages)

deviation score	number in group	hospital admissions		out-patient visits		GP consulted for serious or persistent problem	current health problems	
		nil	3 or more	nil	8 or more		nil	4 or more
males								
nil	101	58.4	6.9	43.7	18.8	24.8	18.8	35.0
one	55	65.5	7.3	21.8	27.3	32.7	14.5	25.0
two	33	45.5	9.1	24.2	39.4	30.3	30.3	10.0
three	19	36.8	–	15.8	36.8	31.6	36.8	1.7
four or five	16	56.2	6.3	12.5	37.5	25.0	–	8.3
six or more	10	70.0	10.0	–	20.0	20.0	10.0	8.3
no parent's form	12	50.0	8.3	8.3	33.3	50.0	8.3	11.7
all males	246	56.5	6.9	24.4	26.8	28.9	18.7	24.4
females								
nil	109	64.3	8.3	52.5	21.1	21.1	21.1	23.9
one	50	40.0	6.0	50.0	14.0	22.0	8.0	30.0
two	28	39.3	17.9	50.0	10.7	17.9	10.7	17.9
three	10	20.0	20.0	20.0	10.0	40.0	–	70.0
four or five	18	27.8	5.6	22.2	16.7	38.9	5.6	38.9
six or more	10	60.0	10.0	70.0	10.0	10.0	20.0	30.0
no parent's form	13	46.2	15.4	46.2	15.4	30.8	23.1	38.5
all females	238	45.8	9.7	46.6	16.8	23.1	15.1	28.6

As we have already seen the number of children evincing a particular type of behaviour problem at nine years of age was often very small. Attempts to use such data to predict later manifestations of ill health are therefore fraught with difficulty and indeed could be misleading. Even if we limit our concern to those types of behaviour reported of at least ten children of the appropriate sex, however, very few signs appear of any association with later ill-health measured in terms of use of health facilities. If we look at three indices of such usage, that is admission to hospital (excluding normal childbirth), more than eight out-patient visits for any reason, and treatment by the family doctor for a persistent or serious problem, as *Table 45* shows, most of those said to have specific behaviour problems at nine conform very closely to the picture of usage manifested by their sex group as a whole. For example 43 per cent of the total male group had been admitted to hospital at least once: the only behaviour traits where the proportion exceeded 52 per cent were those who were said to have cried frequently, those who had frequent headaches as children, and those with very small appetites. Marked under-usage of hospital beds appeared only among those who had disliked school and those who had been described as 'very jealous'. These last two groups are also the least likely to have made frequent out-patient visits while those who disliked school were also least likely to have been treated by their family doctor. This might be interpreted either as demonstrating that those who disliked school at nine were healthier than normal or that they had a tendency to avoid official intervention in their affairs. The number involved is, in any case, so small as to make minor fluctuations appear more important than they warrant.

The men most likely to have made a lot of out-patient visits were those who had frequent nightmares as boys. Those who had cried a lot were again in the 'top' three of attenders as were frequent bedwetters. So far as other behaviour problems were concerned variation from the group figure was small. This was also true of use of the family doctor to cope with persistent or serious problems where only those who had been afraid of the dark and

Table 45 Individual types of behaviour shown by ten or more boys/girls at nine years by use of health resources (percentages)

behaviour at nine years	males				females			
	number in group	hospital admission (%)	more than 7 in-patient visits (%)	persistent problem treated by GP (%)	number in group	hospital admission (%)	more than 7 in-patient visits (%)	persistent problem treated by GP (%)
whole group	246	43	27	29	238	54	17	23
afraid of dark	29	41	35	52	17	62	18	41
dislikes school	10	20	10	10	fewer than 10 cases			
very irritable	25	48	24	24	24	63	8	33
food fads	49	41	35	29	41	51	12	20
small appetite	25	60	32	32	24	38	17	17
often worried	15	47	33	40	13	62	17	31
very restless	53	45	25	26	28	61	23	29
very jealous	10	30	10	20	14	50	11	43
disobedient	27	52	30	19	26	58	nil	27
mood swings	11	46	27	36	10	60	8	40
poor reader	52	37	33	29	25	72	20	28
complains a lot	fewer than 10 cases				17	35	24	29
temper tantrums at least once a week	18	50	28	11	21	57	nil	14

continued

Table 45—continued

behaviour at nine years	males				females			
	number in group	hospital admission (%)	more than 7 in-patient visits (%)	persistent problem treated by GP (%)	number in group	hospital admission (%)	more than 7 in-patient visits (%)	persistent problem treated by GP (%)
quarrelling with other children at least once a month	17	35	29	35	17	71	24	24
crying several times a week	16	63	38	13	28	54	18	18
nightmares more than once a month	21	52	52	33	fewer than 10 cases			
bedwetting more than once a month	13	54	38	31	fewer than 10 cases			
headaches at least once a month	21	57	33	33	29	66	17	28
stomach pain at least once a month	14	36	14	21	25	72	20	24

those often worried showed more than very minor upward fluctuations from the group norm. Downward variation was not only manifested by those who disliked school, as already mentioned, but also by those who had been given to frequent temper tantrums or, strangely, in view of their previous over-representation, those prone to tears.

Among the women, it was also difficult to see any particular relationship between individual behaviour traits at nine and later use of health resources. If we ignore normal confinements, the most likely to have used hospital facilities – both in-patient and out-patient – were those said to be having difficulty in learning to read and those who had quarrelled frequently with other children. Perhaps more logically, those who had suffered from frequent 'tummy pains' or to a lesser extent headaches as young girls, also made above-average use of in-patient facilities but neither group varied much from the norm in terms of frequency of out-patient visits or GP consultations.

Those women *least* likely to be admitted to hospital were those said by their parents to whine or complain a lot as children and these, together with the very jealous, were also least likely to have made frequent use of out-patient clinics. The very jealous, however, compensated for this by being the most likely to have a 'persistent or serious problem' treated by their family doctor, closely followed by those who had been afraid of the dark and those most subject to mood swings. No behaviour group showed marked under-usage of the family doctor.

In considering these findings, it must be remembered that no attempt has been made to differentiate use of health service facilities in terms of *cause*, that is all admissions and visits have been grouped together and treated as equal. It might be argued, however, that this is an oversimplification and that some health problems might bear a greater relationship to 'type of person' concerned than others. Unfortunately the very small numbers involved in most specific types of illnesses (for example psychiatric) make it virtually impossible to establish meaningful relationships. There is, however, one important aspect of *demand* on health facilities which does involve substantial numbers and which may well relate to behaviour and personality – accidental injury. As we have seen this accounts for a large number of the men who have sought hospital treatment and, because of its importance, it is examined in detail in the next chapter.

— 6 —————

WELL-BEING AND PROBLEMS

WELL-BEING

One of the most striking findings of the survey was the satisfaction which respondents felt about their lives at the age of twenty-six. This emerges clearly from *Table 46* which shows that more than 80 per cent of each sex declared that they were at least 'mostly satisfied' with their health and physical condition, what they were accomplishing, and the amount of fun and enjoyment they had, while more than 80 per cent of women and 70 per cent of men were also satisfied (or better) with their family life, their accommodation, and their leisure activities with their family. (In part, at least, these minor sex differences may reflect the lower proportion of married men in the study group.)

Table 40 Well-being at twenty-six by sex

how do you feel about?	females								males							
	delighted	pleased	mostly satisfied	mixed or neutral	mostly dis-satisfied	unhappy	terrible	not answered, not relevant	delighted	pleased	mostly satisfied	mixed or neutral	mostly dis-satisfied	unhappy	terrible	not answered, not relevant
yourself, what you are accomplishing and the way you handle problems?	9 (3.8)	80 (33.6)	104 (43.7)	35 (14.7)	4 (1.7)	3 (1.3)	1 (0.4)	2 (0.8)	11 (4.5)	78 (31.7)	116 (47.2)	30 (12.2)	3 (1.2)	– (–)	2 (0.8)	6 (2.4)
your own family life – your husband/wife, your family, your children?	73 (30.7)	87 (36.6)	44 (18.5)	13 (5.5)	1 (0.4)	1 (0.4)	1 (0.4)	18 (7.6)	53 (21.5)	87 (35.4)	40 (16.3)	18 (7.3)	3 (1.2)	1 (0.4)	– (–)	44 (17.9)
the income you (and your family) have?	9 (3.8)	65 (27.3)	95 (39.9)	43 (18.1)	12 (5.0)	5 (2.1)	8 (3.4)	1 (0.4)	13 (5.3)	52 (21.1)	97 (39.4)	41 (16.6)	23 (9.3)	9 (3.7)	6 (2.4)	5 (2.0)
the amount of fun and enjoyment you have?	30 (12.6)	80 (33.6)	85 (35.7)	29 (12.2)	12 (5.0)	2 (0.8)	– (–)	– (–)	33 (13.4)	88 (35.8)	87 (35.4)	21 (8.5)	7 (2.8)	4 (1.6)	1 (0.4)	5 (2.0)
your house or flat?	49 (20.6)	89 (37.4)	60 (25.2)	16 (6.7)	13 (5.5)	8 (3.4)	2 (0.8)	1 (0.4)	32 (13.0)	70 (28.5)	82 (33.3)	26 (10.6)	12 (4.9)	7 (2.8)	8 (3.3)	9 (3.7)
the things you and your family do?	32 (13.4)	95 (39.9)	80 (33.6)	16 (6.7)	4 (1.7)	2 (0.8)	– (–)	9 (3.8)	18 (7.3)	84 (34.1)	83 (33.7)	32 (13.0)	3 (1.2)	– (–)	1 (0.4)	25 (10.2)
the amount of time you have for doing what you want to do?	7 (2.9)	45 (18.9)	99 (41.6)	39 (16.4)	36 (15.1)	10 (4.2)	2 (0.8)	– (–)	20 (8.1)	49 (19.9)	63 (25.6)	56 (22.8)	37 (15.0)	14 (5.7)	4 (1.6)	3 (1.2)
the way you spend your spare time, your non-working activities?	13 (5.5)	73 (30.7)	97 (40.8)	32 (13.4)	14 (5.9)	4 (1.7)	– (–)	6 (2.5)	14 (5.7)	85 (34.6)	92 (37.4)	32 (13.0)	13 (5.3)	1 (0.4)	3 (1.2)	6 (2.4)
what our government is doing?	1 (0.4)	6 (2.5)	40 (16.8)	106 (44.5)	47 (19.7)	14 (5.9)	18 (7.6)	6 (2.5)	1 (0.4)	11 (4.5)	34 (13.8)	98 (39.8)	40 (16.3)	30 (12.2)	26 (10.6)	6 (2.4)
the goods and services you can buy in this area – things like food, clothes, appliances?	14 (5.9)	39 (16.4)	107 (45.0)	37 (15.5)	28 (11.8)	5 (2.1)	3 (1.3)	5 (2.1)	7 (2.8)	52 (21.1)	94 (38.2)	41 (16.7)	29 (11.8)	6 (2.4)	9 (3.7)	8 (3.3)
your own health and physical condition?	28 (11.8)	119 (50.0)	58 (24.4)	20 (8.4)	8 (3.4)	2 (0.8)	– (–)	3 (1.3)	51 (20.7)	97 (39.4)	66 (26.8)	20 (8.1)	6 (2.4)	1 (0.4)	– (–)	8 (3.3)
your job?	36 (15.1)	73 (30.7)	52 (21.8)	31 (13.0)	5 (2.1)	– (–)	3 (1.3)	38 (16.0)	34 (13.8)	88 (35.8)	68 (27.6)	34 (13.8)	7 (2.8)	4 (1.6)	4 (1.6)	7 (2.8)

In contrast to this the proportion of people expressing dissatisfaction or worse with any aspect of their lives reached as high as 10 per cent on only five items: income, accommodation, free-time, local shopping opportunities, and 'what our government is doing'. The last item was particularly interesting in that the pattern of responses was almost diametrically opposed to that on all the other items with only 20 per cent of women and 19 per cent of men declaring themselves at least 'mostly satisfied'. It is the only item about which more than 7 per cent of respondents said they felt 'terrible' (while only one man and one woman were 'delighted'). In relation to the more personal aspects of life, the main source of dissatisfaction was lack of time 'to do what you want to do' – possibly reflecting the reverse side of family life!

This aura of satisfaction was also evident in the answers to questions about feelings towards different aspects of current *work*. *Table 47* looks at the situation of those who had paid jobs (full- or part-time) or were in full-time education (that is it excludes eighty-nine women and one man who were currently occupied entirely as homemakers and child-carers for their families) and shows, once again, that the majority of people were, at least, 'mostly satisfied' with their working situation. Furthermore, sex differences were small, relating mainly to small differences of emphasis (such as the higher proportion of men who saw themselves as 'pleased' with their working conditions while women were more likely to describe themselves as 'mostly satisfied'). If, however, we group together all those expressing positive views ('mostly satisfied' or better) we find that these small differences are cancelled out so that in four of the eight items (those involving conditions, pay, hours, and immediate boss) men and women are within 1 per cent of each other. The items showing the highest sex differences relate to job prospects (found at least satisfactory by 63.3 per cent of men but only 45.0 per cent of working women) and physical demands made by the job (where 66.2 per cent of men were satisfied but only 55.1 per cent of women).

One of the causes of sex differences in satisfaction appears to relate to lack of relevance of the question rather than to active

Table 47 Attitudes to aspects of paid employment by sex

how do you feel about?	females								males							
	delighted	pleased	mostly satisfied	mixed or neutral	mostly dis-satisfied	unhappy	terrible	not answered, not relevant	delighted	pleased	mostly satisfied	mixed or neutral	mostly dis-satisfied	unhappy	terrible	not answered, not relevant
working conditions (the kind of place you work in)?	26 (10.6)	69 (28.2)	73 (29.8)	39 (15.9)	20 (8.2)	4 (1.6)	7 (2.9)	7 (2.9)	14 (9.4)	26 (17.4)	62 (41.6)	21 (14.2)	6 (4.0)	1 (0.6)	3 (2.0)	16 (10.7)
the hours you work?	25 (10.2)	88 (35.9)	72 (29.4)	30 (12.2)	12 (4.9)	6 (2.5)	8 (3.3)	4 (1.6)	13 (8.7)	49 (32.9)	52 (34.9)	11 (7.4)	5 (3.4)	3 (2.0)	1 (0.7)	15 (10.1)
the physical demands the job makes on you?	22 (9.0)	56 (22.9)	84 (34.3)	49 (20.0)	4 (1.6)	5 (2.0)	7 (2.9)	18 (7.3)	5 (3.4)	25 (16.8)	52 (34.9)	35 (23.4)	3 (2.0)	4 (2.7)	1 (0.7)	24 (16.1)
the mental demands?	14 (5.7)	68 (27.8)	71 (29.0)	52 (21.2)	8 (3.3)	6 (2.4)	4 (1.6)	22 (9.0)	5 (3.4)	34 (22.8)	43 (28.9)	32 (21.5)	4 (2.7)	3 (2.0)	2 (1.3)	26 (17.4)
your workmates (the people you see most often at work)?	37 (15.1)	98 (40.0)	62 (25.3)	24 (9.8)	9 (3.7)	1 (0.4)	3 (1.2)	11 (4.5)	23 (15.4)	55 (36.9)	33 (22.1)	15 (10.1)	4 (2.7)	– (–)	1 (0.7)	18 (12.1)
your immediate boss?	40 (16.3)	60 (24.5)	67 (27.3)	32 (13.1)	12 (4.9)	7 (2.9)	8 (3.3)	19 (7.8)	17 (11.4)	49 (32.9)	36 (24.2)	15 (10.1)	6 (4.0)	9 (6.0)	2 (1.3)	16 (10.7)
your pay?	25 (10.2)	49 (20.0)	76 (31.0)	38 (15.5)	29 (11.8)	11 (4.5)	11 (4.5)	6 (2.4)	10 (6.7)	42 (28.2)	39 (26.2)	18 (12.1)	11 (7.4)	9 (6.0)	4 (2.7)	16 (10.7)
your work prospects?	21 (8.6)	84 (34.3)	50 (20.4)	37 (15.1)	15 (6.1)	13 (5.3)	10 (4.1)	15 (6.1)	11 (7.4)	32 (21.5)	24 (16.1)	23 (15.4)	9 (6.0)	3 (2.0)	5 (3.4)	42 (28.2)

dissatisfaction being greater among the women. This is particularly marked in relation to job prospects where 28 per cent of working women felt that the question did not apply to them (but only 6 per cent of men). As *Table 47* shows, smaller but often still quite substantial differences occurred also in other items. This probably relates to differences in working conditions between women (particularly part-time workers) and men. They may well be the only worker (for example in small shops or in domestic or office cleaning jobs) and hence cannot answer a question about workmates; if they carry out their work at home (for example self-employed, piece-work, or family business where they live 'over the shop') questions about hours of work or conditions in the workplace may present problems.

The other aspect of life explored in detail involved attitudes to domestic tasks. This was felt to be of considerable importance as a source of well-being (or otherwise) for women in the age-group of our sample, many of whom were currently spending the greatest part of their time caring for their home, husband, and young children (see also Chapter 4). Some men also answered these questions, feeling that they played some part, at least, in domestic tasks but, as they were not routinely answered by (or indeed, asked of) all men, the analysis has been limited to female respondents.

As we have already seen in Chapter 4, women who had partners and/or children as well as jobs enjoyed 'being a housewife' rather less than those who were full-time homemakers. In *Table 48* we are comparing full-time homemakers with a slightly different group – that is those who were occupied full-time or part-time outside the home, including single women (since they might have their own flats or participate in domestic work in the parental home or other shared accommodation).

Both groups seemed relatively satisfied with their chores but, on most items, the full-time homemakers felt more positively. Indeed, the only task for which the employed women felt more enthusiasm was 'cooking for special occasions' which 12 per cent of 'housewives' said they disliked (perhaps because of the demands

Table 48 *Women and job satisfaction in the home (percentages based on totals excluding 'not applicable' categories)*

how do you you feel about?	women employed full- or part-time			full-time homemakers		
	at least satisfied	mixed/ neutral	dis- satisfied or worse	at least satisfied	mixed/ neutral	dis- satisfied or worse
doing the housework (cleaning, polishing, etc)?	80 (57.1)	31 (22.1)	29 (20.7)	60 (68.2)	23 (26.1)	5 (5.7)
everyday cooking for the family?	93 (71.0)	25 (19.1)	13 (9.9)	65 (73.0)	21 (23.6)	3 (3.4)
cooking for special occasions	118 (87.4)	9 (6.7)	8 (5.9)	67 (77.9)	9 (10.5)	10 (11.6)
organizing the family finances?	86 (69.4)	23 (18.5)	15 (12.1)	55 (72.4)	14 (18.4)	7 (9.2)
shopping for food and necessaries?	84 (60.4)	35 (25.2)	20 (14.4)	52 (60.5)	19 (22.1)	15 (17.4)
being at home most of the time?	32 (51.6)	8 (12.9)	22 (35.5)	59 (66.3)	16 (18.0)	14 (15.7)
looking after your children when they are babies	40 (78.4)	7 (13.7)	4 (7.8)	77 (92.8)	5 (6.0)	1 (1.2)
looking after toddlers?	43 (87.8)	4 (8.2)	2 (4.1)	65 (85.5)	11 (14.5)	– (–)

of young children). As might be expected, the employed group (or, at least, those of them who did not feel the question wholly irrelevant) were markedly more likely to dislike being at home most of the time. In general, however, the order of liking for different tasks was remarkably similar in each group with care of babies and toddlers and (as already said) 'special occasion cooking' making up the most satisfying tasks while being at home most of the time, everyday shopping, cleaning, and polishing were the least likely to be so described. It is interesting, however, that only a few homemakers said they actually disliked house-cleaning whereas one in five of those employed did so.

Comparing the two groups of women in terms of the general 'quality of life' items (as shown in *Table 46*) revealed surprisingly few differences. If we look at the proportions saying they were at least 'mostly satisfied' in each case, then only in five items were there differences of more than 2 or 3 per cent between the figures for each group. The exceptions were *family life* (95.5 per cent of homemakers; 90.8 per cent of employed women after exclusion of single childless ones); the amount of *fun* and *enjoyment* experienced (84.3 per cent of homemakers satisfied compared with 80.5 per cent of the employed); *accommodation* (87.6 per cent of homemakers; 80.5 per cent of employed); *health* (91.0 per cent of homemakers; but only 83.2 per cent of those employed) and, the only case in which the relationship was reversed, *income* (73.8 per cent of employed women found this satisfactory compared with 66.3 per cent of non-employed). On the whole then the women who were in employment appear to have been marginally less satisfied with their lot than those who were occupied only at home. The differences are small, however, and it must be remembered that the working group included women with broken marriages and also those with larger families (see *Table 32*, p. 83) that is people who may be working *because* of family problems or pressures.

PROBLEMS

Despite their apparent satisfaction with life at the time of the survey, our respondents had not been without trouble in their lives. Asked about 'serious' problems of various types (see *Table 49*), approximately three out of every five people (58.1 per cent of men; 63.9 per cent of women) said they had been affected by at least one while 8 per cent of women and 6 per cent of men mentioned four or more.

Table 49 *Type of problems reported by sex*

	males			females		
	number	% of total	% of those at risk	number	% of total	% of those at risk
serious housing difficulties	47	19.1	19.1	40	16.8	16.8
serious financial problems	51	20.7	20.7	42	17.6	17.6
serious worries involving their children	18	7.3	18.9	24	10.1	18.5
serious worries involving spouse's health or welfare	30	12.2	19.6	31	13.0	14.9
serious worries involving parents' health and welfare	63	25.6	25.6	84	35.3	35.3
serious marital problems, broken engagements, and so on	39	15.9	15.9	47	19.7	19.7
other serious problems affecting life	27	11.0	11.0	19	8.0	8.0

Not only were the number of problems reported very similar in each sex, so were the types. Indeed, the only area involving more than a very minor fluctuation was that which caused the most concern in each sex, that is worries involving *parents' health and welfare*. This was mentioned by one in three of female respondents and one in four of male. The sex difference here is, perhaps, not unexpected in view of the higher demands placed on daughters in terms of care of ailing parents. In fact, it might be expected to be larger and probably would become so as time passed. At the time of the survey, however, many of these parents were still relatively young. When our respondents were born, 63 per cent of their mothers and 41 per cent of their fathers were under thirty years old. Twenty-six years on, therefore, they were still in their late forties or early fifties and not yet prey to the infirmities of old age. One factor which did relate to worries about parents was, however, the death of one of them. Where both parents were alive, only 22 per cent of men and 30 per cent of women said they had experienced some worry; where one parent had died this rose to 62 per cent among the women and 45 per cent among the men. Unfortunately – on the basis of available data – it is not possible to say whether the 'worry' reported related to the actual death of one parent or to concern for the other.

Problems concerning the *health or welfare of their children* were mentioned by just under one in five of those who had any. Among the men, the occurrence of such worries seemed to reflect the number of children in the family so that, while only 10 per cent of those with one child mentioned a problem, this doubled to 21 per cent among those with two children, and went up to 40 per cent where there were three or more. This might perhaps be expected in terms of each child carrying an equal (and independent) 'risk' but for female respondents the rise was much less marked (17 per cent for those with one child and those with two; 27 per cent for larger families). Marital breakdown has already been discussed in Chapter 4 but it is interesting to note here, as a check on accuracy, that those with a 'broken' first marriage were almost unanimous in saying they had experienced 'serious marital problems'. The exceptions were the woman who had been widowed (and who had remarried happily) and one divorced man and one separated woman who did not appear to see the parting from their first partner as problematic. Of those whose first marriages were still intact, 10 per cent of each sex reported serious problems either in that marriage or in some previous relationship while 15 per cent of men and 13 per cent of women not yet married reported the breakdown of 'engagements' and other stable relationships.

Little, unfortunately, can be said about those quite substantial minorities who had experienced worries involving their *spouse's health or welfare* or *financial difficulties*. *Serious housing difficulties* can, however be related to housing type and this showed that those living in local authority housing at the age of twenty-six were much more likely to have experienced such difficulties (56 per cent of men; 41 per cent of women) than were owner-occupiers (8 per cent of men; 7 per cent of women). This marked relationship between housing problems and local authority tenancy undoubtedly reflects the problems of access to such housing. In most areas where local authority housing is in relatively short supply, allocation is on a 'points' basis in which factors such as size of family, defects in existing housing, and overcrowding all contribute to the total score and movement up the waiting-list. Couples waiting for their first 'council house' might therefore experience quite a lot of privation and inconvenience in the interim period.

Attempts to relate childhood behaviour to the propensity to encounter problem areas in adult life yielded little in the way of consistent relationships. Among the women, those with the highest deviation scores at nine (that is three or more) were the least likely to have remained problem-free (eight out of thirty-eight, or 21 per cent) but there was variation within this group with the chance of meeting a problem being greater among those with a score of three (90 per cent) than among those with higher ones (75 per cent). Among those who *had* problems, the people with a deviation score of four or more were among the *most* likely to have more than one (66.7 per cent) but they were closely followed by the deviation-free (where 65.2 per cent of those with one problem also had at least one other).

Among the men, the relationship of deviation to problems differed quite markedly from that among the women so that, while those with a deviation score of three were still the least likely to be problem-free (21.1 per cent), the reverse was true of those with scores of four or more where 53.8 per cent reported no problems and of those who *did* only 25 per cent had encountered more than one (the lowest 'repeat' rate of any deviation group). Perhaps one of the most interesting groups among the men, however, consisted of those whose parents failed to complete questionnaires in 1961, more than half (58.3 per cent) of whom reported *multiple* problems compared with 28.2 per cent of those with forms. This relationship did not pertain among the women where those with questionnaires in 1961 showed a similar profile to those without.

Relating deviation scores to individual problem areas showed little apart from a slight tendency (slight in view of the small number involved) for the men who had no parental questionnaires at nine years old to report more problems with parents, housing, and welfare and health of spouse than did those without.

LIFE NOT WORTH LIVING?

Only a minority of people (23.5 per cent of women; 13.8 per cent of men) admitted that they had ever felt life was not worth living and, of these, just over half (12.2 per cent of women; 8.9 per cent of men) had considered the possibility of ending it. For most, however, this was as far as the matter went: only thirteen women and five men said they had actually tried to kill themselves.

As might be expected, the tendency to see life as not worth living was closely linked to the presence of 'problem' areas in the respondent's life so that 88 per cent of men affected, and 85 per cent of women, had undergone at least one of the problems shown in *Table 49* compared with only just over half (53.3 per cent of men; 57.1 per cent of women) who had never experienced such feelings. Put another way, the proportion feeling life not worth living of men who had experienced three or more different problem areas in life was more than six times as great as among those who had been problem-free (25.7 per cent compared with 3.9 per cent). A similar picture pertained among the women where 59.4 per cent of women with at least three problems had considered life not worth living compared with only 9.3 per cent of those with none.

The likelihood that such feelings arise as reactions to specific happenings, rather than from any basic personality disorder observable in childhood, is reinforced by looking at behavioural deviations reported by parents. Among the men, the total deviation score was *inversely* related to negative feelings in later life; 15.4 per cent of those with no deviant behaviour traits, or only one, had experienced such feelings but only *one* man (2.2 per cent) out of those (forty-five) who had deviation scores of three or more. The men markedly most likely to be afflicted were those whose parents had not completed the original questionnaire (41.7 per cent of whom felt life had been not worth living).

Among the women the distribution was (inverted) U-shaped with those of moderate deviation (that is three to five items) in childhood more likely to have experienced dejection (42.9 per cent) than those at either extreme (18.8 per cent of those free from deviation; 20.0 per cent of those with scores over five). No relationship occurred here with absence of an original parents' form (30.8 per cent reported adverse feelings). Relating the feelings that life was not worth living to individual types of childhood behaviour obviously presented considerable problems because of the smallness of many behavioural categories. If, however, among the men, we limit analysis to behaviour shown by at least eight boys, we find that the behaviour categories in which *no-one* reported ever feeling life not worth living fell into two groups: first, those who were very irritable, very jealous, and very moody, always whining and complaining, cried fequently, and indulged in frequent tantrums (had we adopted a lower cut-off point this group would also have included the very destructive, liars, truants, and those said to sulk very frequently – all of which seem to bear a certain similarity to those listed); second, those who were often worried, were afraid of the dark, and/or had frequent headaches

The men *most* likely to report suicidal feelings were those described as boys as 'very placid' (24.2 per cent) and/or being thumb-suckers (21.4 per cent) but in neither case is the rise much above that expected in terms of the group as a whole.

Among the women, where more had been affected by dejection, all types of behaviour with *any* cases (except 'very destructive') produced at least one person who had felt life not worth living.

The groups with the *lowest* proportion affected, however, still comprised the very irritable (only 8.3 per cent) and the very jealous (14.3 per cent). In general, however, among the women, the tendency was for those who had had behaviour problems *of any kind* to be more likely than average to report feelings of alienation. In general, however, the variation from the norm was small and, if we again exclude categories with fewer than eight cases only one type of behaviour – mood swings (40 per cent affected) showed a frequency more than 10 per cent above the norm.

INVOLVEMENT IN CRIMINAL PROCEEDINGS

Two out of every five male respondents (41.5 per cent) said that they had appeared at least once in court because they had broken the law. As might be expected from national figures, the proportion of women affected was much smaller (6.3 per cent) and almost entirely accounted for by involvement in minor traffic offences. Such offences – for example parking in a restricted area, causing an obstruction, having defective lights/brakes, exceeding the speed limit – also predominated among the men. More serious driving offences (such as dangerous driving, driving under the influence of drink/drugs, driving while disqualified/uninsured) were less common with only fifteen men involved and no women.

Among non-traffic offences (conventional 'crimes') stealing (including robbery, burglary, and shop-lifting, as it was not possible to differentiate on the basis of the information given) predominated and, indeed, was the only 'crime' admitted to by female respondents. Violence towards other people had led to court appearances at least once for only 5 per cent of the men and, as *Table 50* shows, other offences were relatively uncommon. It is also noteworthy that, despite public perceptions of the 'swinging sixties' and the politically active young of the 1970s, only one person said he had appeared in court because of participation in a political protest and two because of drug charges.

Table 50   *Types of crime reported by sex (in order of frequency)*

offence type	males		females
minor traffic offences	63	(25.6)	11
stealing	21	(8.5)	2
serious driving offences	15	(6.1)	–
violence towards other people	11	(4.5)	–
disorderly behaviour	7	(2.8)	–
causing damage to property	4	(1.6)	–
fraud/forgery	3	(1.2)	–
drug related	2	(0.8)	–
political (e.g. related to protest)	1	(0.4)	–
other (including those unclassified because of lack of information	7	(2.8)	2

The 'miscellaneous' category includes two cases of failure to produce a TV licence (one male, one female), one of breaking a probation order (male), one for failing to attend school (female), and five where information about some or all crimes committed was insufficient to allow for classification.

In considering this overall picture we must, however, bear in mind that the same individual can appear in court in connection with different types of crimes or, indeed, may have appeared more than once for the same reason. For example, one man estimated that since he was first brought to court (for burglary) at the age of thirteen, he had been tried on about twenty-five other charges (involving 'violence, theft, criminal damage, drinking and driving, taking and driving'). Another, originally from the same school, who admitted to 'various' (unspecified) reasons for court appearances said he had just completed his second prison sentence and commented that his was 'Quite what people would call a bad record').

Table 51 shows that, of the men who reported prosecutions, nearly half (47 per cent) reported that they had been charged with more than one offence. This does not necessarily mean that they appeared in court more than once, however, since the same incident might involve more than one charge. For example a single

Table 51   *Total number of offences (all ages) reported*

	nil	1	2	3	4	5–9	more than 20	not known
males	144	54	22	8	10	5	2	1
% of offenders	–	52.9	21.6	7.8	9.8	4.9	2.0	1.0
females	223	14	–	–	–	–	–	1
% of offenders	–	93.3	–	–	–	–	–	6.7

'joy-riding' episode could lead to a court appearance not only on the grounds of 'taking' the car but also of driving while uninsured and driving without a licence.

The women, with one possible exception where no details were given of the 'crimes' concerned, reported only single incidents – mainly, as we have seen, involving minor traffic offences. This is not unexpected. Similar large sex differences are to be found in national and international statistics. The reasons given range from the more law-abiding 'nature' of women (inborn or conditioned) to differential treatment by the law. It has also been suggested that the differing life-styles of men and women make male crimes more 'public' and noticeable, those of females more 'private'. For instance, stealing a car may be seen as more 'public' and more likely to involve the police directly than is stealing from the local shop (where the owner may wish to handle the matter in some way other than prosecution). We did not ask our informants to report any illegal activities in which they had participated but only on those for which they were actually prosecuted and so, unfortunately, cannot contribute usefully to such discussion.

It was true, however, that men were likely to have made a court appearance at a younger age than were women. Of women with court appearances, eleven out of fifteen (73.3 per cent) did so for the first time after their twenty-first birthday but this was true of only 28 out of 102 (27.5 per cent) of the male offenders. Conversely 11 out of 102 (10.9 per cent) of males appeared before they were sixteen but only one girl (for failing to attend school).

As might be expected from the overall figures shown in *Table 50*, the majority of those appearing in court on one single occasion did so because of relatively minor traffic infringements (66.7 per cent of female single offenders; 60.0 per cent of male). This was particularly marked among those women whose sole prosecution occurred in adult life (that is over the age of seventeen) where only three of the thirteen women concerned appeared for other causes. Among the men, minor traffic offences accounted for nearly two out of three (63.4 per cent) of those who made their single court appearance in adult life and, perhaps a little surprisingly, half of those whose first and only prosecution occurred before they were eighteen.

Among those forty-seven males whose first appearance was to be followed by one or more others, motoring offences were still important (covering 51 per cent of first offences) but stealing also came into prominence so that fourteen multiple offenders (29.8 per cent) started out as thieves and five (10.6 per cent) with violence against other people. Among those whose criminal career started earliest, theft assumed the greatest importance. *All* ten males who reported two or more offences and whose first appearance had been prior to their sixteenth birthday said that their first court appearance related to stealing of some kind. For those whose court appearances started between sixteen and seventeen, stealing, violence towards others, and motoring offences assumed equal importance (29 per cent in each case). Those reporting multiple offences whose first 'crime' occurred at eighteen or older almost entirely started with driving offences (eighteen out of twenty-one, or 85.7 per cent).

Among the men, age at first court appearance related strongly to whether or not the first charge was accompanied by or was a precursor to others. Thus, of those eleven boys whose first appearance in court occurred before the age of sixteen, only one (9 per cent) reported that this concerned his one and only offence. Among those who were first charged between sixteen and twenty years, the proportion with single offences rose to nearly half (twenty-nine out of sixty-one, or 48 per cent), and among those prosecuted first after their twenty-first birthday only six out of twenty-eight (21 per cent) had faced other charges.

So far as *type of offence* was concerned, those whose first court appearance involved charges of stealing or violence against people were considerably less likely to report that this was the only charge they had ever faced than were those summoned for driving offences (26 per cent of those whose first court appearance was for theft and 29 per cent of those where it was for violence compared with 63 per cent of traffic offenders).

Moving on to consider the most *recent* court appearance of those reporting more than one offence, a relationship to age again becomes evident. Thus of men reporting court appearances relating to more than two offences, only two out of twenty-five (8 per cent) had made their last appearance before the age of twenty-one. This would indicate that those appearing in court over the age of twenty (fifty-four people) may include the more persistent and serious 'criminals'. This is clearly shown by the number of offences reported by this group, that is five (9 per cent) admitted to five or more offences; fifteen (28 per cent) to three or four offences and only twenty-two (41 per cent) were single offenders.

Relating number of crimes to type of the most recent offence indicated that traffic offences tended to be 'one-off' incidents and not related to other types of crimes so that for forty out of sixty-eight (59 per cent) of those whose most recent offence related to traffic infringement, this was their only crime. Otherwise it was difficult to relate number of offences to type of crime with which most recently charged. In part this may well relate to haziness of detail by those with the longest list of convictions; in part it seemed to stem from a lack of specialization among these same persistent offenders. This is shown in the example cited previously where the respondent's 'criminal career' included convictions for personal violence, theft, and driving offences.

In the light of previous research and, indeed, of public opinion, it might be expected that criminal involvement could be predicted

from earlier problems of behaviour. As none of our respondents
had appeared in court before the original survey when they were
nine years old and as their behaviour at home and school had been
examined in some detail then, our data provided an excellent
opportunity to assess how far extent and type of deviating
behaviour could be used to predict subsequent involvement with
the judicial system

As *Table 52* shows, the number of atypical traits reported by
parents when the respondents were nine years old had no value
whatsoever in predicting a delinquent future. Indeed, so far as the
boys were concerned, the best indicator for this purpose was having a parent who refused to complete questionnaires about their
children!

The total score of 'problems' reported by teachers also failed to
demonstrate any clear-cut relationship. Certainly among the
eleven boys with most problems (four or more), six (54.5 per cent)
had subsequently appeared in court – but so had 54 out of 121
(44.6 per cent) of those with *no* problems recorded whereas in the
intermediate range the proportion dropped to approximately a
third (thirteen out of forty) of those with two or three problems
and 40 per cent of those with only one.

Table 52 *Total number of deviating behaviour traits reported by parents when*
respondent aged nine by subsequent appearance in criminal court

number of deviating traits reported	males		females	
	no court appearances	1 or more court appearances	no court appearances	1 or more court appearances
none	64 (63.4)	37 (36.6)	101 (92.7)	8 (7.3)
one	31 (56.4)	24 (43.6)	48 (96.0)	2 (4.0)
two	19 (57.6)	14 (42.4)	26 (92.9)	2 (7.1)
three	7 (36.8)	12 (63.2)	10 (100.0)	– (–)
four or five	13 (81.3)	3 (18.8)	17 (94.4)	1 (5.6)
six to fifteen	6 (60.0)	4 (40.0)	9 (90.0)	1 (10.0)
no form completed	3 (25.0)	9 (75.0)	12 (92.3)	1 (7.7)

Clearly one reason for this lack of association could lie in the different dimensions of behaviour included in the total 'problem behaviour' scores so that frightened children, aggressive children, emotionally unstable children, and troublesome children are all lumped in together.

To obviate this problem a further analysis was carried out which concentrated solely on those children whose behaviour could be seen as involving potentially law-breaking aspects, that is stealing, truancy, wandering from home, destructiveness, and habitual lying. All of these were covered by the parents' questionnaire and two − stealing and lying − by the teachers also.

In *Table 53*, this overall delinquency score is related to subsequent involvement in criminal proceedings and, among the males, a clear association emerges with those with high scores more than twice as likely to appear in court as those with low. Among the women, however, the proportion appearing in court bore little relationship to the manifestation of 'delinquent' behaviour at home or school when they were nine years old. One reason for this almost certainly pertains to the nature of the 'crimes' concerned. Women, as we have already seen, tended in the main to appear in court because of minor traffic infringements, men for a wider range of 'crimes'. In *Table 54* then our delinquency score is related to court appearances for differing types of crimes committed by the men. This shows that involvement in

Table 53 *Delinquent behaviour reported by parents and or teachers at nine years of age by subsequent court appearance(s)*

number of delinquent items of behaviour reported	males		females	
	no court appearances	1 or more court appearances	no court appearances	1 or more court appearances
none	130 (61.3)	82 (38.7)	199 (93.9)	13 (6.1)
one or two	10 (50.0)	10 (50.0)	12 (92.3)	1 (7.7)
four or more[1]	3 (21.4)	11 (78.6)	12 (92.3)	1 (7.7)

Note: [1] No-one in either sex had a score of 3.

Table 54 *Type of crime leading to a court appearance by delinquency score at nine years (males only)*

reason for court appearance	delinquency score at nine years		
	nil	1 or 2	4 or more
violence against people	7 (3.3)	1 (5.0)	3 (21.4)
theft	20 (9.4)	3 (15.0)	4 (28.6)
minor traffic offences	56 (26.4)	4 (20.0)	3 (21.4)
major driving offences	11 (5.2)	3 (15.0)	1 (7.1)

minor traffic offences remained more or less constant in all three delinquency score groups. In comparison theft and violence showed a clear trend (though numbers involved are very small particularly in the 'extreme' delinquency group). It is also evident that more serious driving offences did not increase among those with the highest score.

Table 55 shows that the relationship between the overall delinquency reported at nine and subsequent court appearance (see *Table 53*) is maintained when age is taken into account, thus those with the highest delinquency scores at nine years of age were more likely to appear in court not only as juveniles and adolescents but also as adults. Having once appeared in court, however, they were not more likely to reappear. In each delinquency score group the proportion reporting only one offence remained relatively static at 55–60 per cent. It also must be said that those with the very worst records, in terms of total number of offences admitted to, were not to be found among those with the highest delinquency scores.

BEING A VICTIM

As well as being more likely to be prosecuted for criminal activity, men were nearly twice as likely as the women to say that they had, themselves, been the victim of someone else's crime at some time in their lives (seventy-five men; thirty-nine women). In the main this was accounted for by having something stolen (fifty-three

Table 55 *Age at court appearance(s) by delinquency score at nine years*

	no extreme items	1–2 extreme items	4+ extreme items
at least one court appearance under the age of eighteen	28 (13.2)	3 (15.0)	7 (50.0)
at least one court appearance at eighteen or older	67 (31.6)	9 (45.0)	9 (64.3)

men; thirty women). The number reporting physical attacks were much smaller (fourteen men; nine women) and of these, five women had suffered sexual attacks.

ACCIDENTAL INJURIES

In Chapter 5 we saw what a predominant role accidental injuries played in bringing people – particularly men – to hospital either as in-patients or for out-patient treatment. By the time they were twenty-six nearly two-thirds of male respondents (62.6 per cent) and one in four of the women (25.2 per cent) had suffered at least one such accident necessitating hospital treatment; 35.8 per cent of men, but only 7.6 per cent of women, reported more than one such incident.

The most frequent types of injury involved, in each sex, broken bones, sprains, bruises, wounds, and lacerations. Only eleven men and one woman suffered from burns, while only four women had been poisoned (including the taking of an overdose).

Where location of accident was known, the women were markedly more likely to mention the home (21 out of 60, or 35.0 per cent, compared with 7 out of 154, or 4.5 per cent of the men). Conversely only one woman mentioned an injury received at work (compared with 21 out of 154, or 13.6 per cent of men). Sports injuries were not mentioned at all by women but those caused by vehicles accounted for a marginally higher proportion of women (17 out of 60, or 28.3 per cent of those injured compared with 31 out of 154, or 20.1 per cent of men).

Clearly in terms of numbers injured and even more markedly in terms of numbers involved *repeatedly* the men presented a more interesting group for the study of 'accident proneness' so a more detailed analysis was made of their data.

Unfortunately this could not include information about any involvement in accidents *before* the age of nine. At the time of the original enquiry our attention was focused on 'normal' childhood behaviour and the large-scale events (such as family break-up) which might be associated with any deviations from the 'normal' pattern. Thus, while we collected information about hospital admissions (which involved separation) we did not ask about injuries involving out-patient treatment by hospital, clinic, or general practitioner. Since fewer than five children had been admitted to hospital for reasons which might have indicated accidental injury before the age of ten, it is therefore impossible to say whether or not 'accident proneness' starts early in life. Certainly, however, early hospitalization experiences – for any reason – showed no relationship whatsoever to later involvement in accidents.

The information gathered when informants were twenty-six showed that most of the accidental injuries reported had taken place during adolescence and early adult life (see *Table 56*). Only five of our male respondents said they had been involved in one or more accidents between the ages of nine and fourteen. The proportion injured over the next six years doubled before beginning to fall again in the twenties. It is also noteworthy that the likelihood of being involved in more than one accident within a given age-range rose as the respondents got older. Furthermore, as is shown in the 'all-ages' column in *Table 56*, there was a considerable carry-over from one age group to another. Only ninety-two people (just over a third) remained accident-free at all ages up to twenty-six, with a further sixty-six experiencing only one episode. The remaining eighty-eight (36

Table 56   *Number of accidents by age of occurrence (males)*

number of accidents during age range	age range			all ages
	9–14	*15–20*	*21+*	*9–26*
none	197 (80.1)	146 (59.3)	161 (65.4)	92 (37.4)
one	35 (14.2)	60 (24.4)	47 (19.1)	66 (26.8)
two	8 (3.3)	23 (9.3)	17 (6.9)	34 (13.8)
three or four	3 (1.2)	9 (3.7)	11 (4.5)	29 (11.8)
five or more	– (–)	1 (0.4)	4 (1.6)	17 (6.9)
more than one but number not known	3 (1.2)	7 (2.8)	6 (2.4)	8 (3.3)
total with accidents	49 (19.9)	100 (40.6)	85 (34.6)	154 (62.6)

per cent) reappeared more than once either in the same age group or at an older age.

Few people required in-patient treatment. Excluding those kept in for less than twelve hours or overnight only forty-six men (30 per cent of those with injuries) were admitted to hospital because of their injuries, eleven (7 per cent) on more than one occasion (for different injuries). Most people (119 out of 154, or 77 per cent) received their treatment as out-patients, with the number of attendances *per accident* remaining remarkably constant (at approximately 1.7) regardless of the number of accidents in which the individuals were involved. Clearly, however, in terms of *total* use of casualty and out-patient departments those who had the largest number of accidents were those who created the greatest demands for resources.

Under what circumstances did people come by their injuries? Unfortunately not all informants provided sufficient details to make a comprehensive survey of causes possible. For instance 'broke leg in fall' could have involved a loose rug at home, a ladder at work, a banana skin in the street, or an over-enthusiastic tackle on the sports field. For those (sixty-six) who did provide some detail, however, accidents involving vehicles were the main cause of injury (thirty-one), followed by injuries received on the sports field (twenty-three) and those occurring at work (twenty-one).

Only a relatively small number of men specifically described their injury as having occurred at home. It may be, however, that this picture merely reflects the way in which people describe their experiences. Injuries suffered in public places may be described more in terms of their location (perhaps because of official intervention stressing this aspect) whereas injuries received at home, being 'private' and not usually involving others, may be described in terms of type of injury (for example, 'cut hand' rather than 'cut hand while slicing bread in kitchen'). It is not possible to make any definitive statements of the basis of our data. Bearing in mind its limitations it is, however, interesting to note that the vast majority of those involved in 'traffic' accidents were involved on only one occasion (84 per cent) while, among those injured while participating in sport, 43 per cent had been injured more than once on the sports field. Among those injured at work the proportion suffering repeats in the working environment rose to 62 per cent.

Was there any evidence that accident-prone men could be predicted when they were younger? It has already been said that admission to hospital had no effect whatsoever – and this was true of those who entered hospital in their first year (fourteen), those who were admitted between one and four (thirty-two), and those who were of school age at the time (sixty-five).

As we have already seen (pp. 72–3) very few of our respondents were reported to have experienced atypical family situations in terms of disruption before the age of nine. Looking at attributes of the 'normal' families in which they lived there was some evidence that family size and the social status of the family did bear some relationship to involvement in accidents. Those whose fathers were in manual occupations in 1961 were rather more likely to have been injured since then (92 out of 140, or 65.7 per cent) and those of non-manual fathers (forty-nine out of ninety, or 54.4 per cent). Differences *within* the manual and non-manual group are small. If however, we look at those reporting the most involvement in accidents (that is three or more episodes) we find that those whose fathers were in the upper ranges of non-manual employment (professional, managerial, or executive jobs) were markedly less likely to be represented than were those in other groups. Only two men (3.8 per cent) of those with fathers in the highest status group had been in three or more accidents between the ages of nine and twenty-six; for those with fathers in routine white-collar jobs the proportion rose to 18.4 per cent, and for those in skilled manual occupations to 26.3 per cent. This was the peak – among the sons of semi-skilled or unskilled workers, the proportions dropped again to 17.2 per cent. By far the most accident prone, however, were those whose father's occupation in 1961 was unknown (mainly comprising those whose parents did not complete the questionnaire at all at that time but who themselves provided information at follow-up). Among this group, of sixteen people only three (18.8 per cent) remained totally injury-free and six (37.5 per cent) had suffered at least three accidents.

So far as family composition was concerned there was no evidence that boys from large families were more likely to be involved in at least one accident than were those from small: for all known sizes of family, from one to six or more children, the proportion accident-free remained at between 35 and 40 per cent. Among those who did have at least one accident, however, there were some differences relating to the extremes of family size. Thus, among only children (at least up to the age of nine), two-thirds of those with accidental injuries had been involved in only one accident, two people (13.3 per cent) in three or more such episodes. Among those with five or more siblings the proportions were almost reversed with only 27.3 per cent of those injured reporting a single accident and 54.5 per cent reporting at least three accidents. For the intermediate family sizes, those with between two and five children, the picture remained relatively static with about 40 per cent of those injured reporting only one accident and about 30 per cent three or more. In families with more than one child (in 1961), family position showed no relationship to liability to accidental injury.

Looking at personal traits in terms of problematic behaviour at home at the age of nine, little emerged in terms of our crude 'deviation score'. At the extremes, those boys whose behaviour was absolutely 'normal' according to their parents were rather less likely to get involved in any accidents than were those with one or more deviating traits (48.5 per cent to 31.1 per cent). There was no variation in the proportion free of accidents as the number of deviating behaviour traits reported rose. Those with the highest deviation scores did, however, get involved in *more* accidents: so that, of the twenty-six boys with deviation scores of four or more, 36 per cent reported at least three accidents compared with 16.3 per cent of the others (and there was little variation within the 'other' group).

The number of behaviour problems reported by teachers showed even less relationship to involvement in accidents. Of those with no problems, 38 per cent were accident-free; of those with three or more problems, 40 per cent. Similarly, while 36 per cent of those with most school problems (three or more) had been involved in multiple accidents (two or more) so had 39 per cent of those said to be problem-free.

Relationships in terms of specific types of behaviour reported by parents were more interesting. The 'delinquency' items (very destructive, lying, stealing, wandering from home, and truancy from school) were each, in themselves, too small to make analysis meaningful but when they were combined it became evident that those whose parents said they showed one or more such type of 'delinquent' behaviour at nine years of age were much more likely to become involved in an accident later. Of the twenty-four males in this group only four (16.7 per cent) were still free of any accidental injuries at twenty-six years of age compared with 39.6 per cent of other men.

Another group found to be more 'accident-prone' than normal comprised those men who as children were said by their parents to manifest 'difficult' emotional behaviour (that is extreme irritability, jealousy, or mood swings or frequent – taken as more than once a month – crying, sulking, or temper tantrums). As with the 'delinquent' behaviour, the individual types of behaviour all indicated some association to accidents but numbers, in most cases, were very small. Grouping again, however, produced eighty-eight males who were reported to have shown at least one of these types of behaviour and, again, this group were more likely to have been involved in one or more accidents by the age of twenty-six (71.6 per cent compared with 57.6 per cent of the others.

Both these groups were also more likely to report *multiple* accidents. Thus nearly half of the 'delinquent' group involved in accidents (47.4 per cent) mentioned three or more episodes; for the 'difficult' group, the proportion was 40.7 per cent; while, for the whole group of respondents (see *Table 56*), the figure was only 29.9 per cent.

Reports on classroom behaviour by teachers showed very little association to later accidental injury. Individual items, on the whole, were again too small for meaningful analysis but two groups were constructed similar to those found useful among the parents. One comprised the two 'delinquent' items (that is lying and stealing); the other dealt with emotional reactions (irritability, tantrums in class, moodiness, aggressive behaviour to other children, and crying). Neither showed any predictive value. Thus, of the twenty-eight boys said by teachers to manifest at least one form of problematic emotional behaviour (and only five had more than one) 57 per cent had later been involved in one or more accidents; for those with no such problems, the figure was 63.3 per cent. The thirteen people who were said to lie and/or steal by their teachers at nine were marginally more likely to have an accident (69.2 per cent) than other men (62.2 per cent) but the parents' attributions of delinquency and of 'difficult' emotional behaviour were in each case better as predictions of accident involvement.

The relationship between accidental injury and delinquency, however, did not rest solely on parental reports. Looking at self-reported court appearances (see *Table 57*) we can see that the people reporting the most accidental injuries were also more likely to report appearances in the criminal court so that nearly twice the proportion of men with three or more accidents had

Table 57 *Number of accidents leading to own injury by age of first court appearance*

number of accidents	first court appearance		number with one or more court appearance at any age
	before 18	18 or older	
none (N = 92)	8 (8.7)	20 (21.7)	28 (30.4)
one (N = 66)	9 (13.6)	17 (25.8)	26 (39.4)
two (N = 34)	4 (11.8)	13 (38.2)	17 (50.0)
three or more (N = 46)	15 (32.6)	12 (26.1)	27 (58.7)
number not known (N = 8)	2 (25.0)	3 (37.5)	5 (62.5)

appeared in court as had those who were accident-free. Further-more, looking at the picture in terms of age at *first* court appearance, we can see that the high accident group were very much more likely to say that their first court appearance had occurred before the age of eighteen.

Many individual types of criminal behaviour occurred too rarely to make for meaningful analysis. It was felt, however, that the relationship between accidental injury and prosecutions for traffic violations might be worth pursuing. This proved interest-ing. Prosecutions for major driving offences (for example danger-ous driving) showed no relationship either to reporting *no* accidental injuries (33.3 per cent of those with major traffic viola-tions; 37.7 per cent of those without) or to reporting more than one (traffic violations 33.3 per cent; others 35.9 per cent). *Minor* traffic infringements (for example illegal parking, defective lights, exceeding speed limit) were a different story, however. Here only 27 per cent of offenders were accident-free compared with 41 per cent of non-offenders and the offenders were also more likely to have suffered more than one accident (44.4 per cent compared with 32.8 per cent of those with no minor traffic violations).

The final question which must be asked about accidents refers to alcohol consumption. We have no information about respond-ents' sobriety at the actual time of the accident. We did, however, ask more general questions about the frequency of respondents' drinking at the time of the follow-up. This showed that the few (nineteen) men who never (or very rarely) drank were no more likely to have remained completely free of accidental injuries (36.8 per cent) than were those who drank frequently (38.5 per cent) or occasionally (36.1 per cent). They were, however, less likely to have *more* than one accident in which they were injured (15.8 per cent to 35.4 per cent of those drinking often and 40.2 per cent of those saying they were occasional drinkers).

— 7

CONCLUSIONS

The study described in this book was undertaken with the primary objective of examining the relationship which might exist between children's behaviour, as reported by parents and teachers, at the age of nine and later aspects of those same children's lives as they moved into adulthood. As those who have read the preceding chapters will realize, however, the book has actually developed in quite a different way: it has acquired more breadth and is now predominantly a description of their lives to date given by a group of people aged twenty-six.

This change of emphasis should, perhaps, constitute a source of embarrassment. The study was undertaken because it could relate two sets of contemporary information – that gathered at the age of nine and that reported in adult life – and avoid the pitfalls of faulty recall. In the event, many of the findings reported are based on information supplied restrospectively, for example about education, health, and criminal convictions. To have avoided the use of this material because of its suspect validity would, however, have prevented exploration of some of the interesting relationships which were emerging and emerging very prominently.

Perhaps the clearest example of this lies in the different experiences of men and women, starting in school and continuing into work experiences and attitudes. This showed clearly that, from the time they left primary school, the 'opportunities' of boys were different from those of girls of apparently similar ability. In exploring this phenomenon the starting-point lay in the 1961 data since this provided the teachers' assessments of early ability but, thereafter, in exploring the process of differentiation (in terms of qualifications gained for example) reliance had to be placed on the retrospective information supplied by respondents themselves during the 1978 survey. To have failed to use this material, however, would have made it impossible to show the progression of events by which the females 'lost out' at every step of the way from secondary school selection to career prospects at the age of twenty-six.

In face of such pronounced trends, the analysis of outcome in terms of behavioural anomalies at the age of nine has tended to fade into virtual insignificance. It must not be thought that it was totally ignored, however. Massive and lengthy efforts were made, employing increasingly complex analytical tools, to establish some relationship between outcome and childhood behaviour measured in terms of 'deviation score' (parents), total 'problem score' (teachers), and the individual types of behaviour. Where any relationship existed this has been reported but, as will have been obvious, there was no evidence that those who had manifested the most behavioural anomalies at nine were less successful in later life or that particular behaviour traits had adverse prognostic value. Indeed, so far as total deviation score was concerned the main difference to emerge was between those who were perceived as completely 'normal' at nine and *all* the others.

This is of some importance. Had the survey adopted a different approach and compared only the most deviating group in 1961 with a matched group of those of similar age and sex but 'deviation-free', differences in outcome would have emerged. These would almost certainly have been seen as associated with the earlier deviation so that the high scorers would have been seen as 'different'. It is only with the inclusion of *all* grades of deviation that it becomes clear that the 'very deviating' may differ little from those with only one or two problems.

One reason for the lack of any consistent relationship between total scores and problems in later life could lie in the number of different types of behaviour covered by the 1961 questionnaires and included in these totals. This could mean that we were aggregating as 'high' or 'low' scorers people with very different behaviour patterns. If, however, we look at specific types of behaviour, we still find a lack of association with developing patterns of life.

This lack of association could mean that no association exists between a person's behaviour at nine and what happens later. Children, however odd, may be 'going through a phase' (as many parents believe) and other things being equal (for instance type of education), may suffer no handicap in later life. *Absence* of association is very difficult to establish, however, since it could be explained in terms of faulty methodology. There are various such possibilities.

WERE THE RIGHT QUESTIONS ASKED?

This is difficult to answer since 'right' involves a subjective assessment. Certainly we tried to include a wide spectrum of questions covering most aspects of the informants' lives. As a result, perhaps the questions could be seen as too superficial. Had we devoted less space to employment and more to instruments for measuring psychic state, more relationships might have emerged – perhaps not! This is a topic on which readers will have their own ideas. It must be remembered, however, that some gaps emerged only *after* analysis of the existing data.

WERE THE MOST 'INTERESTING' CASES LOST
THROUGH FAILURE IN TRACING AND RESPONSE?

The question of bias arising because of the loss of approximately a quarter of the follow-up group has already been dealt with in Chapter 1. From the 1961 data available there was no evidence that those lost differed much in childhood from those who provided information. This means that even widespread deviation among them by the age of twenty-six (though interesting in itself) would have had little effect on our findings relating behaviour at nine to later happenings.

One subgroup does call for comment, however. This comprises the people whose parents were also non-respondents in 1961. Obviously little is known about these people. We do know, however, that in 1961 those whose parents did not complete questionnaires were more likely to manifest academic and behavioural problems *in school*. There is therefore a possibility that their parental forms, had they been completed, would have disclosed some deviations also. We also know that the twenty-five people who had no parental questionnaire but who provided information themselves in 1978 showed an increased tendency to have encountered problems in their lives. This is particularly so among the twelve men concerned, who were more likely to have appeared in court, more likely to have suffered accidental injury, more likely to say that they had encountered multiple problems in their lives, and more likely, perhaps as a result, to have felt that life was 'not worth living'. None of these differences applied to the women but both they and the men were more likely to report frequent job changes.

Clearly it would be very foolish to argue from such a small number of cases but, nevertheless, there does seem to be a possibility that non-response may have affected results. It is, however, the non-response of 1961 rather than that of 1978 which has caused the problem. In the light of this we can only say that parental failure to provide any information about a child seems to carry a more adverse prognosis than declaration of even multiple behavioural deviations.

WAS THE COVERAGE ADEQUATE IN TERMS
OF PEOPLE?

This is perhaps the most crucial question. In Chapter 1 we outlined the reasons for selecting the study group in terms of age
rather than by extent of behavioural anomaly. This decision was
justified by our finding that while those with many deviations
might differ from those with none they did not show any consistent surplus of 'problems' of any kind over those with lower
scores (see p. 148). The decision to limit coverage to a specific age
group, however, limited total numbers to those included in the
original survey (that is 10 per cent of appropriately aged pupils).
Since these children were a cross-section of the population,
obviously, this reduced the number who would manifest marked
behaviour deviation of any kind either in childhood or later. The
childhood situation was known – hence the original idea of
selecting by deviation score *across* age groups to obtain sufficient
cases for analysis. The 'normality' of our group as they moved
into adult life was less expected. It does, however, point to the
necessity for a very large number of cases being included in
follow-up studies of this kind. Here, we started with a 10 per cent
sample of an entire age group living in a quite extensive geographical area and yet it was not sufficient for us to make a meaningful
comparison of the occurrence of relatively rare events in the lives
of those concerned. An increased coverage (had it been possible in
terms of the original data) might well have improved the
sharpness of analysis – it would certainly have increased the cost
of the exercise, and this provides one of the classic dilemmas of
social research.

In the light of these difficulties perhaps this study should be
seen as providing the groundwork for future more detailed work
rather than as supplying any definitive answers. It has failed to
provide any grounds for predicting the future on the basis of
nine-year-olds' behavioural characteristics when other factors
such as sex, educational attainment, and socio-economic
background are held constant. It does, however, provide a group

'case history' – a picture of what happened to a particular group of children of the 1960s as they moved through life to become the young adults (and, indeed, parents) of the late 1970s.

It must be stressed, however, that it is not possible to generalize from their experiences. Originally as nine-year-olds they were a random sample of their peers. As such they were, at least, representative of other children of their age living in Buckinghamshire. By the time they reached twenty-six this was no longer true. Many, as we have seen, had moved to other places and even other countries. Furthermore, the population of the area had changed as people from outside moved in and some of the changes had been extensive – for example the development of the new town of Milton Keynes and the changes in the racial mix of the population. This makes it difficult to generalize from our findings. Had we taken a random sample of twenty-six-year-olds living in the same area in 1978, the picture might not be quite the same. If we had chosen a comparable group living in Tyneside, Liverpool, or the Glasgow area it would almost certainly have differed widely – particularly in terms of employment factors and housing. Had we even postponed the follow-up for a few years, the picture might have been very different. No shadow of widespread unemployment had as yet touched these people in 1978. One or two mention 'redundancy' but in each case new work was readily available – a very different situation from that pertaining even in the 'affluent' south-east in the 1980s. The experiences of our predominantly happy, healthy, and successful informants reflect the period of post-war affluence in Britain. It is a period that is gone but, perhaps, the picture of it that emerges here in the reported experiences of some of those who lived through it will have relevance for historians of the future.

Appendix 1

BUCKINGHAMSHIRE CHILD SURVEY

A

Below are some descriptions of illnesses and health problems which can affect children. If any item is true of your child, will you please put a line under **Yes**. If the item does not apply to your child then please put the line under **No**.

This child

1. Wears glasses always	Yes	No
2. Wears glasses sometimes	Yes	No
3. Is having treatment for eyes at clinic or hospital	Yes	No
4. Has had persistent ear-ache or running ear during the last twelve months	Yes	No
5. Seems to have difficulty in hearing sometimes	Yes	No
6. Has a hearing aid	Yes	No
7. Suffers from sick headaches	Yes	No
8. Gets travel sick in car, bus or train	Yes	No
9. Has frequent colds or sore throats	Yes	No
10. Has a persistent and troublesome cough	Yes	No
11. Is overweight	Yes	No
12. Is underweight	Yes	No
13. Has fainted more than twice in life	Yes	No
14. Is highly strung	Yes	No
15. Has suffered from a rash or other skin trouble which lasted for two weeks or longer	Yes	No
16. Has to wear special support for bone or muscle disorder (for instance, iron on leg, built up shoe, etc.)	Yes	No
17. Has to wear brace on teeth	Yes	No
18. Has a stammer	Yes	No

(continued)

Has a **doctor** ever said that this child suffered from

19. Any disease or disorder of the bones (*Not* a broken bone).......... Yes   No
20. Any disease or disorder affecting muscles .... Yes   No
21. Heart trouble .... Yes   No
22. Eczema.. Yes   No
23. Asthma.. Yes   No
24. Tuberculosis.. Yes   No
25. Any chronic lung trouble (such as chronic Bronchitis) .... Yes   No
26. St. Vitus Dance .... Yes   No
27. Meningitis (Brain Fever).. Yes   No
28. Migraine .... Yes   No
29. Cerebral Palsy ('Spastic')... Yes   No
30. Fits or Convulsions .... Yes   No
31. Diabetes .... Yes   No
32. Rheumatic Fever.. Yes   No
33. Hare-lip or cleft palate .... Yes   No
34. Any disorder of the glands (*not* just swollen neck glands).......... Yes   No
35. Any other physical handicap or **chronic** illness .... Yes   No

   If so, what is it? Please write it below.

   ....

   ....

   ....

For Girls only:
36. Have periods started yet? .... Yes   No

37. At what age was first period (write in number).....................

38. If periods have started, does she
   (a) Worry about it.   *Please underline any*
   (b) Feel sick.   *of these items which*
   (c) Complain of pains.   *you think apply to*
   (d) Have to stay away from school or go to bed.   *this girl*
   (e) Usually have no trouble or worry at all.

For Boys only:
39. Has his voice broken yet? .... Yes   No

40. If so, at what age did this happen?...............

(continued)

41. Has this child ever had any illness or operation which made it necessary to stay in hospital for more than one night?................ Yes No. If so, please fill in the details below.

Age when went to hospital	*How long stayed there*	*Name of illness, accident or operation*
42.	....	....
....	....	....
....	....	....
....	....	....

43. If the child has been in hospital, did you find that behaviour had changed in any way immediately after return home?

    ....
    ....
    ....

44. Has this child ever attended a special school or class because of a health problem (hearing, sight, speech, etc.)? If so, please tell us about it.

    ....
    ....
    ....

B

Below are some statements which describe the way that children behave. In each group of three, please underline the description that best suits *your* child at the present time.

45. Seldom or never purposely destroys things.
    About as destructive as most children of the same age.
    Very destructive.

46. Very much afraid of one or more animals (that is ordinary British animals, not lions, tigers, etc.).
    A little afraid of some animals.
    Not at all afraid of animals.

47. Has no fear of meeting new people.
    A little afraid or shy of new people.
    Generally fearful of unfamiliar people.

(continued)

48. Afraid of the dark when in bed at night.
    Seems a little uneasy unless a dim light is left on.
    Has no fear of the dark.

49. Always tells the truth.
    Tells an occasional fib.
    Tells deliberate untruths quite often.

50. Likes school very much.
    Likes school about as much as most children.
    Dislikes going to school.

51. Never takes anything that belongs to someone else.
    Has helped himself to someone else's things at least once or twice (including taking things belonging to other members of the family).
    Has stolen things on several occasions.

52. Very irritable, easily becomes cross or annoyed.
    Occasionally becomes cross (for instance, if tired or provoked by other children).
    Very placid nature, practically never gets cross or annoyed.

53. Rather fussy about food, will eat only certain things.
    Has fairly definite food preferences but will eat most foods if hungry.
    Will eat nearly anything.

54. Not at all shy, mixes freely with other children.
    A little shy with strange children.
    Very shy, bashful, fearful of other children.

55. Always hungry, eats a great deal both at meals and as snacks between meals. Can't stop him eating.
    Eats about as much as others of the same age.
    Small appetite, inclined to pick at food.

56. Very carefree, doesn't worry about anything.
    Occasionally worries (for instance, about tests at school or illness in the family).
    Often seems worried, worries about many things.

57. Complains and whines a lot, hard to satisfy.
    Complains about as much as most children of the same age.
    Seldom or never complains or whines.

58. Very restless and fidgety, cannot sit still for a minute.
    About as active as most children of the same age.
    Less active than average, likes sitting still as much as possible.

(continued)

59. Tends to be very jealous.
Occasionally shows jealousy.
Seldom or never jealous.

60. Never wanders off from home without saying where going.
Loiters on way home from school or may go to play with friends without telling parents.
Wanders off for long distances or long periods without parents knowing where.

61. Almost daily has times of being drawn into self and out of touch with other people.
Occasionally seems lost in a dream world.
Seldom or never day dreams.

62. Always does things when told.
About as obedient as most children.
Usually resists when asked or told to do things.

63. Plays truant from school more than once or twice a month.
Plays truant more than three to four times a year.
Never plays truant.

64. Has a very noticeable twitch of face or body, or mannerism, which takes place most of the time.
Has occasional twitches or mannerisms which occur when tired, bored, etc.
Has no twitches or mannerisms.

65. Moods very changeable, on top of the world one minute, down the next for no particular reason.
Occasional changes of mood in response to things that happen.
Runs on very even keel, always the same except under very unusual circumstances.

66. Seemed to have difficulty in learning to read.
Learned to read as quickly as most children.
Good reader, learned to read more quickly than other children.

67. Is there anything about your child's behaviour or habits which worries you but which we have not mentioned?

If so, please tell us about it here...

....

....

....

(continued)

Below is a list of minor health problems which most children have at some time. Please tell us how often each of these happens to your child by putting a tick (√) in the appropriate column.

Example. If your child complains of headaches about once a month you would put the tick (√) in column (e) where it says 'About once a month'. If your child has only had a headache once or twice in his or her whole life, then you would put the tick (√) in column (h) where it says 'Never or less than once a year'.

	(a) Every day or almost every day,	(b) Two or three times a week.	(c) About once a week.	(d) About once every two weeks.	(e) About once a month.	(f) About once in two or three months.	(g) Two or three times a year.	(h) Never, or less than once a year.
68. Has constipation … … …								
69. Has headaches … … …								
70. Has nightmares or unpleasant or frightening dreams … …								
71. Is restless in sleep, tosses and turns, kicks off bedclothes, or walks in sleep, etc. … … … …								
72. Wets the bed … … …								
73. Has pains in stomach … …								

(continued)

Example.—Continued

	(a) Every day or almost every day,	(b) Two or three times a week.	(c) About once a week.	(d) About once every two weeks.	(e) About once a month.	(f) About once in two or three months.	(g) Two or three times a year.	(h) Never, or less than once a year.
74. Vomits								
75. Has diarrhea								
76. Poor control of bowels, soils self								
77. Cries								
78. Sulks for hours on end ...								
79. Has real temper tantrums (that is complete loss of temper with shouting, angry movements, etc.) ...								
80. Bites nails								
81. Sucks thumb or finger								
82. Has bitter quarrels with other children								

C

Thank you for telling us about your child. Now, to finish, could you please give us some information about the child's background as this will help us a great deal when we come to compare the answers of all our parents.

83. What was this child's age **last** birthday? ....

84. Is this child a boy or a girl? ....

85. Is the person answering these questions the child's mother? .....   Yes   No
    If not, please explain who it is..

86. How many **other** children are there in the family?..........................Boys

    ....Girls.

87. Is the child's father alive? ....   If so, what is his age? ....

88. Is the child's mother alive?...................   If so, what is her age? ....

89. Is this child
    (*a*) The only one.
    (*b*) The youngest.   *Please underline the description*
    (*c*) The oldest.   *that applies.*
    (*d*) In the middle.

90. What is the name of your husband's job? ....
    Please describe what he does ....
    ....
    ....

91. Besides being a mother, do **you** have a job?
    (*a*)   Full-time?
    (*b*)   Part-time?
    (*c*)   Not at all?

92. How long have you lived in the district in which you live now?
    ....

93. Where did you live before that? (*Just give the name of the town or village* not
    your address)
    ....

(continued)

94. Has either parent been away from home (for instance, in hospital) for more than a month since this child's birth? Yes   No.   If so, was it Father/Mother? *(Please underline right word.)*

95. Apart from any visits to hospital (which you have already described) has the child lived away from home (for instance, with relatives) for more than a month at any one time? If so, please tell us about it.

....

....

....

....

THANK YOU VERY MUCH.

PLEASE DO NOT SIGN YOUR NAME.

Appendix 2

Serial No. ....

BUCKINGHAMSHIRE CHILD SURVEY

Name of child ....

Address ....

School .... Class ....

A. ATTENDANCE

1. Number of attendances credited during last *complete* term ....

2. Total number of possible attendances during that term ....

3. *Please underline* any of the following reasons for absence which you believe apply to this child:
   (a) Genuine illness of child
   (b) Illness of parent or other member of family
   (c) Parental holiday taken during school term
   (d) Periodic visits to hospital, clinic, etc.
   (e) Truanting (absence without parental permission)
   (f) Odd days and half days off for no good reason but apparently with support and knowledge of parents
   (g) Any other reason (please specify) ....

   ....

B. ATTAINMENT

1. Age range in child's class .... 2. Child's age ....

3. Is this child's place in class or teaching group usually in
   (a) Top 25%
   (b) Middle 50%   (*please underline*)
   (c) Bottom 25%

(continued)

4. If there is more than one stream for this age group, is streaming
   - (a)   Parallel
   - (b)   Based on merit   *(please underline)*
   - (c)   Based on month of birth?

   If merit streaming is used, how does this child's class compare with others in

   the same year (e.g. middle of three, second of five, etc.)...............................

   ....

5. *Please underline* in each question below the item which best fits this child:
   - (a)   General attainment level above average for age, and type of school
           General attainment level average for age, and type of school
           General attainment level below average for age, and type of school
   - (b)   Has not yet learned to read
           Reading ability below average for age
           Reading ability average for age
           Reading ability above average for age

6. Has this child been given any intelligence or other standardized tests (for
   instance of reading age) at school? If so, please give details below.

Name of Test	*Child's Age at Test*	*Result (IQ, Reading Age, etc.)*
....	....	....
....	....	....
....	....	....

C.   BEHAVIOUR AND HEALTH PROBLEMS

1. *Please underline*, in the list below, any items which describe this child as he
   often is:
   - (a)   Very restless, can't sit still for a moment
   - (b)   Cries more than most children
   - (c)   Has a stammer
   - (d)   Has other speech difficulty
   - (e)   Often tells lies
   - (f)   Has stolen things on one or more occasions
   - (g)   Is very easily frightened
   - (h)   Bites finger nails
   - (i)   Sucks thumb or finger
   - (j)   Very irritable, easily becomes cross or annoyed
   - (k)   Has had one or more temper tantrums at school during this year
   - (l)   Is unco-operative in class
   - (m)   Very shy, finds it difficult to mix with other children
   - (n)   Has wet or soiled self at school during last year

(continued)

(o)   Has noticeable twitch of face or body
(p)   Worries more than other children
(q)   Aggressive towards other children
(r)   Very quiet or withdrawn
(s)   Very moody – on top of world one minute, down the next
(t)   Not interested in school work
(u)   Has on one or more occasions during this school year shown fear of school – that is, tears on arrival or refusal to come into the building.

2. Has this child, to the best of your knowledge, any medical disability or chronic illness? (Please do *not* ask the child). If so, what is it? Does it affect performance or participation in school activities?

....

....

....

D. Other Comments

If there is any other information about this child which we have not covered but which you feel to be relevant (e.g. home conditions), please use this space to tell us about it.

....

....

....

....

....

....

....

....

....

....

....

....

....

....

....

Appendix 3

BUCKINGHAMSHIRE CHILD SURVEY FOLLOW-UP STUDY

As you were only nine/fourteen years old at the time of the original survey, quite a lot will have happened to you since then. Below are questions about some of these things. Will you please answer them either by writing in the details asked for or, where we have given you answers to choose from, by putting a tick in the box beside the most appropriate answer for you. For instance in question 1 if you left school at sixteen, you would put a tick in the box beside 16 ☑

SECTION A: SCHOOL

1. How old were you when you left school?

   15 ☐   16 ☐   17 ☐   18 ☐   19 ☐

2. What *type* of school was the *last school* you attended?

   comprehensive ☐   secondary modern ☐

   grammar ☐   technical ☐

other (if so, what type of school was it?)...

3. Thinking back to your days at secondary school, will you tell us whether you agree or disagree with the following statements. RING THE NUMBER that most reflects your feelings. For example, if you enjoyed school on the whole ring the figure ①

	agree	disagree	don't know
On the whole I enjoyed being at school	1	2	0
I found school a bit of a bore	2	1	0
I worked pretty hard at school	1	2	0
The things we learned at school were useful preparation for later life	1	2	0
Teachers thought I was a bit of a problem child	2	1	0
I was pretty bright at school	1	2	0

(continued)

	agree	disagree	don't know
I got the impression some teachers didn't think I was worth bothering about	2	1	0
I was a regular attender even in my final year	1	2	0
I used to enjoy having a bit of a giggle in class	2	1	0
I was sorry to leave school	1	2	0

4. Did you get any qualification before you left school?

   O levels? If so, how many? (write in number here) ....

   A levels? If so, how many? (write in number here) ....

   C.S.E.? If so, how many? (write in number here) ....

   Any others (eg. R.S.A., City & Guilds)? If so, please give details ....

   ....

   ....

5. Since you left school, have you undertaken any further education or training?

   YES, full-time ☐ YES, part-time ☐ No ☐

   If YES, please give details of type of course and any qualification gained. Please give as much detail as possible.

   ....

   ....

SECTION B: EMPLOYMENT

6. Have you ever undertaken an apprenticeship of any kind?

   YES ☐   NO ☐

   If YES, please give details ....

   ....

   ....

(continued)

7. How soon after leaving school/college, did you start your first *full-time* job (ie. NOT including part-time or holiday jobs)?

almost immediately ☐   within 3 months ☐   more than 3 months ☐

If you did NOT start work almost immediately was this because:

you wanted to have a holiday/travel first? ☐

there were no suitable jobs available?   ☐

you were waiting for a particular job?   ☐

you were sick?   ☐

any other reason (*please give details*)..

....

8. People have different reasons for choosing jobs. When you chose your FIRST job, which of these reasons do you think applied to you? Please RING the appropriate number in each case.

	YES	NO
It was the kind of work I wanted to do	1	2
It was the first job I was offered	1	2
I'd heard it was a good firm to work for	1	2
My friends worked there	1	2
The starting pay was good	1	2
It had good prospects	1	2
It was the only job available at the time	1	2

Now could you please UNDERLINE the reason which was most important for you. If we have not mentioned your main reason for choosing your first job, please write it in here.

....

....

9. Could you please give us details of the jobs you have had since finishing your full-time education, starting with the first one? Under 'job' please put the TYPE OF WORK you did, NOT the name of the firm. If for any reason (eg. sickness, unemployment, retirement for family reason) you were not working for a period longer than four weeks please show this. If you are (or have been) a full-time housewife, please enter this in the same way as you would an outside job. If you have had *more than eight* jobs please make sure that you tell us about your *first job* and your *present* or *most recent* one.

(continued)

	job	*how long were you there?*	*why did you leave?*
first job:	....	....	....
second:	....	....	....
third:	....	....	....
fourth:	....	....	....
fifth:	....	....	....
sixth:	....	....	....
seventh:	....	....	....
eighth:	....	....	....

SECTION C: MARRIAGE AND FAMILY

10. Are you married? ☐ divorced? ☐ separated? ☐ widowed? ☐

    in a stable relationship with someone? ☐ single? ☐

    If you are, or have been married, how old were you at marriage?........

    If your marriage has broken up or you are widowed, how old were you when this happened?........

11. Do you have children (including step-children or foster children if they live with you as part of your family)?

    YES ☐   NO ☐

    If YES, please give the number of children of each sex and their ages

    ....boys aged........

    ....girls aged........

12. When your family is complete, how many children would you like to have?........

13. If you have children, do you feel that they take after you in their behaviour or personality? If so, in what ways do you see them as being like you? In what ways do they differ from you?

    ....

    ....

(continued)

14. If you have children, have you met any particular problems so far in bringing them up (for example in connection with their health, behaviour, progress at school)?

YES ☐   NO ☐

If YES, could you please describe the problem..

....

15. Does your husband/wife have a job?

YES ☐   NO ☐

If YES, what does he/she do?..

16 Does your total net income (ie take home pay) including that of your spouse/partner come to:

under £60 per week? ☐   £60–£80? ☐   £80–£100? ☐   £100–£150? ☐

More than £150 per week? ☐

17. With your income do you feel that you are:

very well off ☐   relatively well off ☐   about normal ☐

rather badly off ☐   very badly off ☐

18. How much *extra* money (if any) would you say that you needed each week so that you could live free of money worries?........

SECTION D: ACCOMMODATION

19. Do you still live in your parents' home?   YES ☐   NO ☐

    If NO, at what age did you leave home?........

20. If you no longer live in your parents' home, is your present accommodation (please TICK)

    rented from a local authority?   ☐

    provided by or rented from your employer?   ☐

    rented from a private landlord?   ☐

    your own?   ☐

    other?   ☐

(continued)

21. What kind of accommodation are you living in at present?

    detached house ☐   bungalow ☐   semi-detached house ☐

    terraced house ☐   block of flats ☐   flatted house ☐

    room or rooms (self-catering) ☐   lodgings ☐   hotel or hostel ☐

    other (please give details) ....

22. How long have you lived in this accommodation?........

23. How do you feel about your present accommodation?

    Would you say on the whole you were:

    very satisfied? ☐   satisfied?   ☐

    dissatisfied?   ☐   very dissatisfied? ☐

24. How do you feel about the *district* you live in now?

    Would you say on the whole you were:

    very satisfied? ☐   satisfied?   ☐

    dissatisfied?   ☐   very dissatisfied? ☐

25. Who else usually lives with you? Please give details below of your household
    in terms of each person's relationship to *you* (eg wife, daughter, your friends,
    fiancee, etc.). Do *not* put their *names*.

    ....

    ....

SECTION E: PARENTS

26. Did you live with your parents until you left school?

                          YES ☐   NO ☐

    If NO, could you explain? ....

    ....

27. How would you describe your relationship with your parents (or those you
    regarded as 'parents') when you were young?

    Was your relationship with your MOTHER:

    excellent? ☐   good on the whole? ☐   a bit mixed? ☐   rather poor? ☐

    terrible? ☐

(continued)

What about your FATHER? Was your relationship with him:

excellent? ☐　good on the whole? ☐　a bit mixed? ☐　rather poor? ☐
terrible? ☐

28. Which parent did you feel closer to when you were at school?

mother ☐　father ☐　both equally good ☐　neither ☐

29. Are your parents (or those you regard as 'parents') still alive?

father?　YES ☐　　NO ☐

If YES, when did you last see him?........

mother?　YES ☐　　NO ☐

If YES, when did you last see her?........

30. How often do you have contact with your parents now? TICK appropriate spaces in each column

	visits	telephone	letter
daily	....	....	....
several times a week	....	....	....
once a week	....	....	....
at least once a month	....	....	....
5–6 times a year	....	....	....
at least once a year	....	....	....
less often	....	....	....

31. How would you describe your PRESENT relationship with your parents? Please TICK in the appropriate box for each parent.

mother		father	
☐ 1	excellent	☐ 1	
☐ 2	good on the whole	☐ 2	
☐ 3	a bit mixed	☐ 3	
☐ 4	rather poor	☐ 4	
☐ 5	terrible	☐ 5	

SECTION F: HEALTH

One of the aspects of your life we looked at very closely in our original study was your health. Could you just bring us up to date by answering a few questions about how you have been since 1961?

(continued)

32. *Since 1961*, have you had to go into hospital as an *in-patient* (ie staying over-night) for any reason? Please give details below.

	age	hospital name	cause of admission	did you have an operation?	how long were you in?
1	....	....	....	....	....
2	....	....	....	....	....
3	....	....	....	....	....
4	....	....	....	....	....
5	....	....	....	....	....

33. *Since 1961*, have you attended a hospital or other clinic as an *out-patient* (including visits to the casualty department)? (COUNT each *group* of visits as one entry, as in example).

	Age	Hospital	Reason for attending	Clinic	Number of visits
Example	17–20	Barking	X-rays and tests	chest	6 monthly for 3 years. Total *6* visits
1	....	....	....	....	....
2	....	....	....	....	....
3	....	....	....	....	....
4	....	....	....	....	....
5	....	....	....	....	....

34. *Since 1961*, have you had any persistent, serious or worrying health problems which have been treated by your GP (or by anyone else such as an osteo-path)? If so please give details below.

....

....

35. Have you ever felt that you might suffer some form of nervous breakdown?

YES ☐   NO ☐

If YES, when was that? ....

....

36. Now could you please tell us about how you have been feeling in recent weeks. Below is a list of various health troubles or complaints which people

(continued)

sometimes have. Will you TICK in the appropriate column beside each type of illness to tell us whether *in the last few weeks* you have suffered from such a complaint and, if so, whether it troubled you just a little or quite a lot. *For example*, if you had a bit of a cold last week but didn't feel bad enough to go to bed or take time off work, you would tick in the *middle* column. If you had not had a cold for some time, then you would tick in the *first* column.

	not at all	this troubled me a little	this troubled me a lot
colds or flu'	....	....	....
dizziness	....	....	....
general aches and pains	....	....	....
headaches	....	....	....
nervousness or tenseness	....	....	....
rapid heart beat	....	....	....
shortness of breath	....	....	....
skin rash	....	....	....
upset stomach	....	....	....
back pain	....	....	....
difficulty in getting to sleep	....	....	....
waking early and unable to get back to sleep	....	....	....
feeling generally run down	....	....	....
women only: period pains	....	....	....
heavy bleeding	....	....	....
feeling irritable, tense or tearful just before your period	....	....	....

37. *During the last few weeks* have you taken (or are you still taking) any pills or medicines for the following reasons? If you *have* taken such medicine, could you TICK in the appropriate column to show whether it was prescribed for you by a doctor, whether you bought it from the chemist without a prescription, or whether it had been prescribed for someone else with the same problem.

Have you taken anything	nothing	doctor's prescription	bought from chemist	someone else's
to help you sleep at night?	....	....	....	....
as a tonic?	....	....	....	....
for your nerves?	....	....	....	....
to relieve pain?	....	....	....	....
for any other reason? SPECIFY	....	....	....	....

(continued)

38. Do you smoke?   YES ☐   NO ☐

    If YES, frequently? ☐   occasionally? ☐

    If NO, have you ever smoked regularly?   YES ☐   NO ☐

39. Do you drink (alcohol):

    quite often ☐

    only occasionally ☐

    practically never ☐

    never ☐

40. During the last SIX months how many days have you had to take off work or from carrying out your usual activities because of illness or injury?........

    For how many of those days did you have to go to bed?........

SECTION G: PROBLEMS

41. During the course of their lives many people find that they have broken a law and have to appear in court. Has this ever happened to you?

    YES ☐   NO ☐

    If YES, what was that for?........

    How old were you then?........

    What did you get?........

    Was that the only time you had to go to court?

    YES ☐   NO ☐

    If you have been to court on other occasions could you please provide details below.

    ....

42. Have you ever been the victim of an illegal act by someone else?

    YES ☐   NO ☐

    If YES, what was that?   theft ☐   assault ☐   sexual offence ☐

    other (SPECIFY) ....

43. During their lives many people encounter problems of various kinds. Since you were grown up have you ever had any of these problems? Please TICK in the appropriate column.

(continued)

	yes	no	not relevant
serious housing difficulties	....	....	....
serious financial difficulties	....	....	....
serious worries involving your children	....	....	....
serious worries involving your husband's/ wife's health or welfare	....	....	....
serious worries involving your parents' health or welfare	....	....	....
serious marital problems, broken engagements, etc.	....	....	....
any other serious problems which have affected your life	....	....	....

44. Have things ever been so bad that you have felt life was not worth living?

YES ☐   NO ☐

If YES, have you ever thought of ending it all?

YES ☐   NO ☐

If YES, have you thought of ways of doing this?

YES ☐   NO ☐

If YES, have you actually tried?

YES ☐   NO ☐

SECTION H: PERSONAL CHARACTERISTICS AND OUTLOOK

45. Now we would like you to answer some questions about the type of person you are. Below you will find sets of three statements describing the ways that people can feel. Please UNDERLINE, in each set of three, the *one* description which you feel best applies to you. For instance, in the first set, if you were a very shy person, you would underline 'I dislike having to meet strangers'; if you were an outgoing person, you would underline 'I enjoy meeting new people'.
   (a) I enjoy meeting new people
       I am a little shy with people I haven't met before
       I dislike having to meet strangers
   (b) I often feel worried
       I occasionally worry (eg over changes at work or family problems)
       I am very carefree and seldom worry about anything
   (c) I occasionally become irritable (eg if I am tired)
       I am very irritable and easily become annoyed
       I am very even tempered

(continued)

(d) I can't bear to be doing nothing
I like to keep active but don't mind sitting down to relax for an hour or two
I am quite happy to sit and take things easy for as long as I can
(e) I am a very happy person
I often feel very depressed
I am as happy as most people
(f) I have a few close friends
I have lots of friends
I have no real friends
(g) I have very changeable moods – sometimes up, sometimes down, for no particular reason
My moods change in response to things that happen
I have a very even temperament – always much the same except under very unusual circumstances
(h) I like to go to parties where there are lots of people
I prefer my own company or just that of the family
I like small intimate social gatherings
(i) I never lose control of myself when I am angry
I can usually control my anger
I easily lose control when I am angry
(j) I occasionally day-dream
I often get lost in a world of my own
I am very down-to-earth
(k) I am very contented with my life
I am as content as most people
I often feel very discontented

46. Finally, we would like to ask you some questions about how you feel about your life as a whole. As you read each question will you please look at the scale below and write down the *number* on the scale that best describes the way you feel in answer to that question. As you can see the scale runs from 1 'delighted' to 7 'terrible'.

I feel

1	2	3	4	5	6	7

| delighted | pleased | mostly satisfied | mixed (about equally satisfied and dissatisfied) | mostly dissatisfied | unhappy | terrible |

A neutral (neither satisfied nor dissatisfied)
B I have never thought about it
C doesn't apply to me

(continued)

Suppose we asked you 'How do you feel when work is over for the day?' If you felt just great about it, then you would choose ① If you felt a little less pleased you could choose ② and so on. If you really felt 'terrible' about stopping work, then you would put ⑦. You will also see that there are *three* other possible answers – A, B, and C – which people can use – if the question does not apply to them (C); if they have never thought about it (B); or if the question deals with a topic about which they have no feelings at all (A).

IN EACH CASE PLEASE WRITE ON THE LINE TO THE RIGHT OF THE QUESTION, THE NUMBER ON THE SCALE (OR THE LETTER) WHICH BEST DESCRIBES YOUR FEELINGS.

How do you feel about:

yourself – what you are accomplishing and the way you handle problems _____

your own family life – your wife/husband, your marriage, your children _____

the income you (and your family) have _____

the amount of fun and enjoyment you have _____

your house/flat _____

the things you and your family do _____

the amount of time you have for doing the things you want to do _____

the way you spend your spare time, your non-working activities _____

what our government is doing _____

the goods and services you can buy in this area – things like food, clothes, appliances _____

your own health and physical condition _____

your job _____

If you are *employed* or *self-employed*, please answer the following questions about your PRESENT job. If you are *not employed* please answer with respect to your MOST RECENT job.

How do (did) you feel about:

your working conditions (ie the kind of place you work(ed) in)? _____

the hours you work(ed)? _____

the physical demands the job makes (made) on you? _____

the mental demands the job makes (made) on you? _____

your workmates (the people you see (saw) most often at work)? _____

your immediate boss? _____

your pay? _____

your prospects? _____

INDEX